CIF PUBLIC SECTOR SUB-CONTRACTS

EXPLAINED

CIF PUBLIC SECTOR SUB-CONTRACTS

EXPLAINED

By
James Howley
&
Martin Lang

CLARUS PRESS

Published by
Clarus Press Ltd,
Griffith Campus,
South Circular Road,
Dublin 8.

Typeset by
Compuscript Ltd,
Shannon Industrial Estate,
Shannon,
Co. Clare.

Printed by
E-Print Ltd, Dublin

Front Cover Photography
Aerial photo of Dublin City Centre
Gerry O'Leary © www.gerryoleary.com

ISBN
978-1-905536-41-2

A CIP catalogue record for this book is available from the British Library.

ABOUT THE AUTHORS

James Howley MSc, Dip Arb, Dip Proj Mgmt, MRICS, FCIOB, FCIArb., Chartered Arbitrator, Chartered Surveyor, Accredited Adjudicator, CIArb Accredited Mediator has over 30 years experience in the construction industry. In addition to building and civil engineering contractors, he has worked with professional consultancy practices. His experience includes large-scale building and civil engineering projects, including utilities, rail, roads, oil and power generating projects in Ireland, the UK, mainland Europe and the Middle East.

He holds an MSc in Construction Law and Arbitration from Kings College, London and has completed formal training in arbitration, adjudication and mediation. He is currently working in private practice as a Construction Contracts Consultant, Arbitrator, Conciliator and Adjudicator.

Martin Lang, MCIArb., CIArb Accredited Mediator, Engineers Ireland Assessed Conciliator, CIArb Assessed Conciliator. Martin is Head of Contracts and Dispute Resolution in the Construction Industry Federation and has been involved in the construction industry for over 35 years with 20 years experience in Senior Management roles in General Contracting, Subcontracting and Civil Engineering projects in Ireland, Europe, the Middle East and Africa.

He is an experienced dispute resolution practitioner and trainer and has dealt with over 200 construction related disputes.

He is the co-author of *Public Works Contract for Building Works Designed by the Employer: Explained* (Clarus Press, Dublin, 2008); *Public Works Contract for Civil Engineering Works Designed by the Employer: Explained* (Clarus Press, Dublin, 2008); and *Minor and Short Forms of Public Works Contracts Designed by the Employer: Explained* (Clarus Press, Dublin, 2009).

PREFACE

CIF Public Sector Sub-Contracts Explained is the fourth book in the "Explained" series. This book is based on and explains the following sub-contracts published by the Construction Industry Federation "Agreement and Conditions of Sub-Contract for use in conjunction with the forms of Main Contract for Public Works Issued by the Department of Finance 2007" and the "Agreement and Conditions of Sub-Contract (NN) for use in conjunction with the Forms of Main Contract for Public Works issued by the Department of Finance 2007 where the Sub-Contractor is a specialist who has been Named by the Employer or whose Contract with the employer has been Novated (NN Sub-Contractor)".

Given that it is generally agreed that public procurement will be the major activity sector of the construction industry for the foreseeable future a large proportion of public sector construction projects will be procured under the Public Works Contracts and the contractual relationships between main contractors and sub-contractors will be critical to both parties for the successful completion of any contract. It is clear that an understanding of the elements involved in these contractual relationships will be at the heart of this success. It is also important that those already involved in public works construction contracts, whether they are designers, engineers, quantity surveyors, consultants, contractors or those setting out on a career in construction, that they have an understanding of how these forms of contracts will impact on the ways in which public works construction projects are executed.

This book explains each contract clause in a clear and easy to understand manner to allow the reader to develop an insight into how these contracts will operate. This book will add to the readers' understanding of the strict and critical administrative procedures demanded by these contracts.

Martin Lang & Jim Howley,

October 2011

CONTENTS

Contents of Part I

Contents of Part II

INTRODUCTION

GENERAL NOTE

AGREEMENT AND CONDITIONS OF SUB-CONTRACT FOR USE IN CONJUNCTION WITH THE FORMS OF MAIN CONTRACT FOR PUBLIC WORKS ISSUED BY THE DEPARTMENT OF FINANCE 2007
MAY 2008

and

AGREEMENT AND CONDITIONS OF SUB-CONTRACT (NN) FOR USE WITH THE FORMS OF MAIN CONTRACT FOR PUBLIC WORKS ISSUED BY THE DEPARTMENT OF FINANCE 2007 WHERE THE SUB-CONTRACTOR IS A SPECIALIST WHO HAS BEEN NAMED BY THE EMPLOYER OR WHOSE CONTRACT WITH THE EMPLOYER HAS BEEN NOVATED ("NN SUB-CONTRACTOR")
1st EDITION FEBRUARY 2008

Both forms of sub-contracts are 'Domestic Type Sub-Contracts' for use with Main Contracts. Both forms are for use with both building and civil engineering contracts.

Sub-contracting — key changes from the (old) Government Departments and Local Authorities (GDLA) sub-contracts

Compensation Event means an event which is so designated in the table in Section K of the Schedule Part 1 of the Main Contract.

Contractor's Risk Event means events where the Contractor retains the risk and where the Sub-Contractor will receive compensation.

Initial Sub-Contract Sum means the sum tendered by the Sub-Contractor and accepted by the Contractor, including any adjustments agreed before acceptance.

Sub-Contractor's Personnel means the employees and other persons, including Sub-Contractors to the Sub-Contractor, working on or adjacent to the Site for the Sub-Contractor or Sub-Contractors to the Sub-Contractor and other persons assisting the Sub-Contractor to perform the Sub-Contract.

Sub-Contractor Risk Event means events where the Sub-Contractor retains the risk and where the Sub-Contractor will not receive compensation.

Sub-Contractor's Things means equipment, facilities and other things the Sub-Contractor [or Sub-Contractor's Personnel] uses on or adjacent to the Site to execute the Sub-Contract Works, except Sub-Contract Works Items.

Sub-Contract Documents means the documents so identified in Article 5 of the Sub-Contract Agreement.

Sub-Contract Sum means the value of the Sub-Contract works calculated in accordance with these Conditions of Sub-Contract.

Sub-Contract Works means that portion of the Works which are to be constructed by the Sub-Contractor including, where applicable, any design to be carried out by the Sub-Contractor.

Sub-Contract Works Item means a part of the Sub-Contract Works, anything that the Sub-Contractor intends will become part of the Sub-Contract Works, or temporary works for the Sub-Contract Works.

Unfixed Sub-Contract Works Items means items of work which have not yet been incorporated in the Works.

Works means the works which are to be constructed under and in accordance with the Main Contract.

Specialist under the Main Contract means any of the following:

- A Sub-Contractor or supplier of a works item named in the contract.
- Contractor's Personnel who do or are to do design.
- Contractor's personnel stated in the Work Requirements to be specialists.

Sub-Contractor under the Main Contract means a person to whom the execution of part of the Works is subcontracted by the Contractor or another Sub-Contractor.

There are no PC Sums or nominated Sub-Contractors, only specialists who will be regarded as 'domestic contractors'.

The Contractor is responsible for the design by Specialists.

There is a provision for professional indemnity insurance.

There is a provision for collateral warranties.

Health and Safety Regulations are reflected in the contract conditions.

The new subcontracts are divided into three parts

- **The Agreement**
- **The Conditions (1–13)**
- **The Appendix Parts 1–4. The appendix will identify the risks applicable to either the Contractor or the Sub-Contractor.**

PART I

AGREEMENT
AND
CONDITIONS OF SUB-CONTRACT

FOR USE IN CONJUNCTION WITH THE FORMS OF MAIN CONTRACT FOR PUBLIC WORKS ISSUED BY THE DEPARTMENT OF FINANCE 2007

This form of sub-contract is issued by the
Construction Industry Federation,
Construction House, Canal Road, Dublin

CONTENTS OF PART I

AGREEMENT

THIS AGREEMENT is made on

BETWEEN:-..

of...

....

(the Contractor)

and...

of...

....

(the Sub-Contractor)

WHEREAS:-

A.   The Contractor has entered or will enter into a Contract (which is defined in the Appendix Part 1) with the Employer for the Works described in the Main Contract.

B.   The Contractor and the Sub-Contractor agree to enter into this Sub-Contract under the terms and conditions herein agreed.

THE CONTRACTOR AND THE SUB-CONTRACTOR AGREE AS FOLLOWS:-

Article 1:   The Sub-Contractor shall execute and complete the Sub-Contract Works and otherwise comply with its obligations in accordance with the Sub-Contract Conditions.

Article 2:   The Contractor shall pay the Sub-Contractor the Sub-Contract Sum subject to and in accordance with the Sub-Contract and shall comply with its other obligations in the Sub-Contract.

Article 3:   The Initial Sub-Contract Sum including VAT is € (
). The Initial Sub-Contract Sum is a lump sum and shall only be adjusted when the Sub-Contract says so.

Article 4:   The Sub-Contractor has satisfied itself before entering into the Sub-Contract of all the circumstances that may affect the cost of executing and completing the Sub-Contract Works and of the correctness and sufficiency of the Initial Sub-Contract Sum to cover the cost of performing the Sub-Contract. The Sub-Contractor has included in the Initial Sub-Contract Sum allowances for all risks, customs, policies, practices, and other circumstances that may affect its performance of the Sub-Contract, whether they could or could not have been foreseen, except for events for which the Sub-Contract provides for adjustment of the Initial Sub-Contract Sum.

Article 5:   The Sub-Contract consists of the following documents:-

- This Agreement;

- The attached Conditions of Sub-Contract and completed Appendix Parts 1 and 2;

- The Main Contract Documents in so far as these relate to the Sub-Contract Works;

- The additional documents identified in the Appendix Part 1 hereto as relating specifically to the Sub-Contract Works;

Present when the Common Seal of THE CONTRACTOR
was affixed hereto:

....

Present when the Common Seal of the SUB-CONTRACTOR
was affixed hereto:

....

OR

Signed by an Authorised Representative of the CONTRACTOR

....

in the presence of .... (Witness)

Address of Witness ....

....

Signed by an Authorised Representative of the SUB-CONTRACTOR

....

in the presence of .... (Witness)

Address of Witness ....

....

NOTE

The first part of the sub-contract sets out the Articles of Agreement. This is the basic Contract and describes what the Sub-Contractor agrees to do and the price the Contractor agrees to pay to the Sub-Contractor. The Articles of Agreement set out the fundamental relationship between the Contractor and the Sub-Contractor.

There are five Articles expressing the Sub-Contract. Between them they establish that in exchange for the Sub-Contract Sum the Sub-Contractor will carry out the Sub-Contract Works in accordance with the Sub-Contract Documents. Article 4 sets out that, in calculating the Initial Sub-Contract Sum the Sub-Contractor has taken into account "allowances for all risks, customs, policies, practices, and other circumstances that may affect its performance of the Sub-Contract, whether they could or could not have been foreseen, except for events for which the Sub-Contract provides for adjustment of the Initial Sub-Contract Sum" unless the Sub-Contract specifies otherwise. The Initial Sub-Contract Sum is inserted as VAT inclusive and is referred to as a lump sum to be adjusted only when the Sub-Contract says so.

CONDITIONS

1. THE SUB-CONTRACT

1(a) Definitions

In this Sub-Contract unless the context otherwise requires:-

Compensation Event means an event which is so designated in the table in Section K of the Schedule Part 1 of the Main Contract.

Contractor's Risk Events are events (if any) which are listed in Section I of the Appendix Part 1. They are events for which compensation is not payable by the Employer under the terms of the Main Contract but in respect of which compensation is payable by the Contractor to the Sub-Contractor.

Initial Sub-Contract Sum means the sum tendered by the Sub-Contractor and accepted by the Contractor, including any adjustments agreed before acceptance.

Sub-Contractor's Personnel means the employees and other persons, including sub-contractors to the Sub-Contractor, working on or adjacent to the Site for the Sub-Contractor or subcontractors to the Sub-Contractor and other persons assisting the Sub-Contractor to perform the Sub-Contract.

Sub-Contractor's Risk Events are events (if any) which are listed in Section J of the Appendix Part 1. They are events for which the Sub-Contractor takes the risk and, if they arise, the Sub-Contractor will not be entitled to compensation (irrespective of whether they are Compensation Events under the Main Contract).

Sub-Contractor's Things means equipment, facilities and other things the Sub-Contractor [or Sub-Contractor's Personnel] uses on or adjacent to the Site to execute the Sub-Contract Works, except Sub-Contract Works Items.

Sub-Contract Documents means the documents so identified in Article 5 of the Sub-Contract Agreement.

Sub-Contract Sum means the value of the Sub-Contract works calculated in accordance with these Conditions of Sub-Contract.

Sub-Contract Works means that portion of the Works which are to be constructed by the Sub-Contractor including, where applicable, any design to be carried out by the Sub-Contractor.

Sub-Contract Works Item means a part of the Sub-Contract Works, anything that the Sub-Contractor intends will become part of the Sub-Contract Works, or temporary works for the Sub-Contract Works.

Unfixed Sub-Contract Works Items means items of work which have not yet been incorporated in the Works.

Works means the works which are to be constructed under and in accordance with the Main Contract.

1(b) Interpretation

(1) The parties intend the Sub-Contract to be given purposeful meaning for efficiency and public benefit generally and as particularly identified in the Sub-Contract.

(2) Words which are defined in clause 1.1 ("Definitions") of the Main Contract will have the same meaning when used in this Sub-Contract as in the Main Contract. The fact that a word is being used in its defined meaning will be indicated by the use of upper case printing in relation to the initial letters, irrespective of whether the words are defined in the Main Contract or the Sub-Contract.

(3)   The words and phrases to which interpretations are ascribed by clause 1.2.2 of the Main Contract have, unless the context indicates otherwise, the same interpretations in this Sub-Contract.

(4)   If the Sub-Contract includes a requirement for the Sub-Contractor to carry out design, the words "execute" and "execution" in respect of the Sub-Contract Works shall be deemed to include design irrespective of whether design is expressly stated or not.

(5)   Reference to any Act of the Oireachtas shall include any Act replacing that Act or amending it, and any Order, Regulation, Instrument, Directions, Scheme or Permission made under it or deriving validity from it.

(6)   The headings and index (including its references to the Main Contract) appearing in this Sub-Contract are for reference purposes only and shall not affect the construction or interpretation of this Sub-Contract.

1(c)   Assignment

The Sub-Contractor may not assign the benefit of the Sub-Contract, or any part of it, without the Contractor's consent.

1(d)   Period of Liability

If the Main Contract is executed under seal, the period of liability of the Sub-Contractor shall be twelve years.

1(e)   Execution of the Sub-Contract Works

The Sub-Contractor shall design (to the extent that this is the Sub-Contractor's responsibility), execute and complete the Sub-Contract Works to the reasonable satisfaction of the Contractor and in conformity with the reasonable directions and requirements of the Contractor.

1(f)   Sub-Contractor's Obligations

(1)   The Sub-Contractor will observe, perform and comply with all of the provisions of the Main Contract in so far as they relate and apply to the Sub-Contract Works (or any portion of the same) and are not repugnant to or inconsistent with the express provisions of this Sub-Contract as if all the same were severally set out herein.

(2)   The Sub-Contractor shall avoid through any neglect, omission or act on its part occasioning the Contractor to be in breach of any of the terms and provisions of the Main Contract. The Sub-Contractor is entitled to a copy of the documents comprising the Main Contract (the **Contract Documents**) in so far as these relate to the Sub-Contract Works. The Sub-Contractor however is not entitled to particulars relating to the Contractor's prices and these may be deleted from any documents to which the Sub-Contractor is entitled.

(3)   The Sub-Contractor will deliver to the Contractor any notice, information or other requirement relating to the Sub-Contract Works, which the Contractor is entitled to or is required to furnish to the Employer's Representative, in sufficient time and detail as to enable the Contractor to meet the time requirements and other obligations of the Main Contract.

1(g)   Damages for breach of the Sub-Contract

In the event that either party is in breach of the Sub-Contract the other party will be entitled to damages suffered as a consequence, provided due notification is given to the other party in accordance with the terms of the Sub-Contract.

> **NOTE**
>
> Clause 1(g) entitles either party to damages arising from a breach of Sub-Contract by the other party.

1(h) Rights and Benefits under the Main Contract

So far as is lawfully permissible, the Contractor will, at the request and cost of the Sub-Contractor, obtain for the Sub-Contractor any rights or benefits of the Main Contract, only in so far as the same are applicable to the Sub-Contract.

1(i) Performance Bond / Sureties

If the Appendix Part 1 requires a Performance Bond, the following shall apply.[*check] Before commencement on site, the Sub-Contractor will procure a bond from an insurance company or a bank approved by the Contractor (such approval not to be unreasonably withheld) guaranteeing the due performance of the Sub-Contract by the Sub-Contractor. The amount of the performance bond will be 25% of the Initial Sub-Contract Sum up to certification by the Employer's Representative of Substantial Completion of the Works and 12.5% of the Initial Sub-Contract Sum for the subsequent 15 months.[*check] The form of the bond will be subject to the approval of the Contractor, such approval not to be unreasonably withheld or delayed.

1(j) Works Requirements

Where the Main Contract is for works designed by the Contractor, the Sub-Contractor is deemed to have satisfied itself before entering the Sub-Contract of the adequacy of the Works Requirements in so far as they relate to the Sub-Contract Works. The Contractor is not liable to the Sub-Contractor for the Works Requirements. The Sub-Contractor however will not be liable to the Contractor for either of the following:-

(i) Statements in the Works Requirements of intended purpose of the Works or parts of them;

(ii) Criteria in the Works Requirements for testing or performance of the completed Works or part of them;

> **NOTE**
>
> This clause sets out the general parameters of the sub-contract and contains similar provisions compared with the existing contract forms: Definitions, Interpretation, Assignment, Period of Liability, Execution of the Sub-Contract Works, Sub-Contractor's Obligations, Rights ands Benefits under the Main Contract, Bonds and Works Requirements.
>
> Sub-clause 1(i) provides the provision for the bond is 25% of the Initial Sub-Contract Sum up to certification of the Substantial Completion of the Works and then reduces to 12.5% of the Initial Sub-Contract Sum for the subsequent 15 months.

2.   THE LAW

2(a)   Law Governing the Contract

Irish Law governs the Sub-Contract and its interpretation.

2(b)   Compliance with Legal Requirements

(1)   The Sub-Contractor shall in performing the Sub-Contract comply with all Legal Requirements.

(2)   The Sub-Contractor shall give and comply with all notices and pay all taxes, fees and charges required under Legal Requirements in connection with performing the Sub-Contract unless the Works Requirements say otherwise. Where such taxes, fees and charges relate in part to the Sub-Contract Works and in part to other works the same will be apportioned proportionately between the Contractor and the Sub-Contractor on a fair and reasonable basis.

2(c)   Consents

The Employer has obtained, or shall obtain the Consents the Works Requirements specify that the Employer is to obtain. The Contractor is obliged under the Main Contract to obtain all other Consents. In so far as such other Consents relate to the Sub-Contract Works, the Sub-Contractor shall obtain those Consents. If the Contractor is obliged to obtain Consents under the Main Contract which are required partly but not exclusively in relation to the Sub-Contract Works or to enable the Sub-Contractor to meet its obligations under this Sub-Contract, the cost of obtaining such Consents will be borne as between the Contractor and the Sub-Contractor on the basis of what is fair and reasonable having regard to the extent to which the Consents relate to the Sub-Contract Works and other works respectively. Any delay, loss or expense incurred by the Contractor and the Sub-Contractor in obtaining or failing to obtain such Consents will be borne in similar proportions respectively.

2(d)   Safety, Health and Welfare Statutory Requirements

(1)   The Sub-Contractor will comply with the Construction Regulations and will provide to the Contractor all documents required for the Safety File (as defined in the Construction Regulations) relevant to the Sub-Contract Works in sufficient time as to enable the Contractor meet its obligations under the Main Contract.

(2)   The Sub-Contractor (without limiting its other obligations) shall ensure, so far as is practicable, that the Sub-Contract Works:-

   (i)   are designed (to the extent that they are designed by the Sub-Contractor or the Sub-Contractor's Personnel) to be safe and are capable of being constructed safely and without risk to health and

   (ii)   are constructed in a safe manner and

   (iii)   are constructed to be safe and without risk to health and

   (iv)   can be maintained safely and without risk to health during use and

   (v)   comply in all respects, as appropriate, with the relevant statutory provisions;

(3)   The Sub-Contractor represents and warrants to the Contractor that the Sub-Contractor is, and will be, while performing this Sub-Contract, a competent person for the purpose of ensuring, so far as is reasonably practicable, that the Sub-Contract Works are as stated in sub-clause 2(d)(1).

NOTE

This clause contains general requirements in relation to compliance with legal requirements, consents and health and safety. It is worth noting that under clause 12.1.1.8, of the Main Contract, any breach of Safety, Health and Welfare statutory requirements is a potential termination event. This applies to all the Contractor's personnel including Specialists and Sub-Contractors.

3. LOSS, DAMAGE AND INJURY

3(a) Sub-Contractor's Indemnities

(1) The Sub-Contractor will indemnify and save harmless the Contractor against and from any loss or expense incurred by the Contractor due to any failure on the part of the Sub-Contractor to observe the terms of this Sub-Contract or the terms of the Main Contract insofar as they apply to this Sub-Contract, including, where applicable, any liquidated damages (or charges made under Clause 7.12 of the Main Contract if applicable) the Contractor is obliged to pay to the Employer as a result of such failure.

(2) The Sub-Contractor will indemnify and save harmless the Contractor and the Employer in relation to any damage to the Works or to any property of the Contractor or of the Employer arising from or in the course of the Sub-Contractor's performance or non-performance of the Sub-Contract. The Sub-Contractor's liability under this sub-clause will not apply to the extent that the loss or damage arises from circumstances to which the Employer's indemnity under clause 3.5 ("Employer's Indemnity") of the Main Contract applies or to the extent that the same was caused by the negligence or default of the Contractor. Nor will the Sub-Contractor be liable for such loss and damage to the extent that it is occasioned by a risk which is that of the Employer under the Main Contract.

(3) The Sub-Contractor will indemnify and save harmless the Contractor and the Employer in respect of any loss arising as a result of:-

   (i) Death, injury or illness of any person; and

   (ii) Loss, destruction of or damage to any physical property; and

   (iii) Obstruction, loss of amenities, nuisance, trespass, stoppage of traffic and infringement of light, other easement or quasi easement;

   arising from or in the course of the performance or non-performance of the Sub-Contract. The Sub-Contractor's indemnity in relation to the death, injury or illness of Sub-Contractor's Personnel will apply regardless of whether the death, illness, or injury was caused wholly or in part by the negligence of the Contractor or any other party, except that if the death, injury or illness was caused solely by the wrongful acts or omissions of the Contractor, its servants or agents, this indemnity to the Contractor will not apply. [*check] Subject to the foregoing the Sub-Contractor will not be liable to indemnify the Contractor or the Employer in respect of the risks identified in sub-clauses (i), (ii) and (iii) above to the extent that the loss is caused by the negligence of the Contractor or the Employer or as a result of the risks in relation to which the Employer has indemnified the Contractor under clause 3.5 ("Employer's Indemnity") of the Main Contract or the risks assumed by the Employer under clauses 3.1 ("Employer's Risks of Loss and Damage to the Works") and 3.8 ("Existing Facilities and Use or Occupation by the Employer") thereof.

3(b) Obligation to Repair

In case of any loss or damage to the Sub-Contract Works, including any Sub-Contract Works Items, due to any event which is at the risk of the Sub-Contractor, including any loss or damage due to defective design by the Sub-Contractor, the Sub-Contractor shall proceed with due diligence to rectify such loss or damage at its own expense.

3(c) Insurance of the Works and Sub-Contractor's Things

(1) The Contractor shall for the benefit of itself and its Sub-Contractors keep in force in accordance with the requirements of the Main Contract a policy of insurance covering the Works

and Works Items (including the Sub-Contract Works and Sub-Contract Works Items) which as regards loss or damage shall be at the sole risk of the Contractor while covered by the said insurance policy.

(2) The Sub-Contractor shall take out insurance on terms and with an insurer approved by the Contractor (such approval not to be unreasonably withheld) of the Sub-Contractor's Things against destruction, loss and damage to their full reinstatement value.

(3) The Sub-Contractor shall be deemed to have knowledge of all terms and conditions in the Contractor's policy of insurance covering the Works and the Sub-Contractor shall be entitled to inspect the said policy upon reasonable notice.[*check] The Sub-Contractor shall observe and comply with the conditions contained in the Contractor's policy of insurance covering the Works in so far as compliance is within the control of the Sub-Contractor. The Sub-Contractor will indemnify the Contractor in relation to any act or omission on the Sub-Contractor's part which causes the Contractor's said policy to become invalid or ineffective in whole or in part.

3(d)   Public Liability and Employer's Liability Insurance

(1) Before commencing the Sub-Contract Works, the Sub-Contractor shall take out with an insurer approved by the Contractor (such approval not to be unreasonably withheld) Public Liability and Employer's Liability policies of insurance as provided herein. The Sub-Contractor will maintain such insurance until the Defects Certificate is issued by the Employer's Representative.

(2) The minimum indemnity limits of these policies shall be the sums stated in the Appendix Part 1 hereto or, if no sums are so stated, shall be those sums stated in the Schedule Part 1D of the Main Contract.

(3) The excesses in the Sub-Contractor's policies of insurance shall not exceed the sums stated in the Appendix Part 1 hereto or, if no sums are so stated shall not exceed the sums stated in the Schedule Part 1D of the Main Contract.

(4) The said policies shall cover the Sub-Contractor's liability under statute and at common law and its liability to indemnify the Contractor under clause 3(a)(3) of this Sub-Contract, except damage to the Works and Works Items which is covered by the insurance policy required to be effected by the Contractor under the provisions of clause 3(c)(1) hereof.

(5) The Sub-Contractor's public liability policy shall be issued in the joint names of the Sub-Contractor, the Contractor and the Employer and will contain cross liability clauses such that the policy shall operate as if a separate policy had been issued to each. If under the Main Contract the Contractor's public liability insurance is required to include as joint insured another party named by the Employer that party will also be a joint insured in the Sub-Contractor public liability insurance policy.

(6) The Sub-Contractor's Employer's liability policy shall include a provision by which in the event of any claim in respect of which the Sub-Contractor would be entitled to receive indemnity under the policy being made against the Contractor or the Employer the insurer will indemnify the Contractor and the Employer against such claims and any costs, charges and expenses in respect thereof.

(7) The Sub-Contractor may only include in its policies under this clause the exclusions permitted by the Main Contract in relation to the insurances taken out by the Main Contractor in so far as the same apply, *mutatis mutandis*, to the Sub-Contractor and / or to the Sub-Contract Work.

3(e)   Professional Indemnity Insurance

If the Appendix Part 1 hereto states that professional indemnity insurance is required in relation to the design of the Sub-Contract Works by the Sub-Contractor, the Sub-Contractor shall arrange such cover for the sum indicated by that Appendix Part 1 to commence with the commencement of the design of the Sub-Contract Works and to remain effective for a period of six years from substantial completion of the Works, unless otherwise stated in the Appendix Part 1 hereto. This insurance shall include retroactive cover to when the Sub-Contractor's design of the Sub-Contract Works and Sub-Contract Works Items started.

3(f) Evidence of Insurance Cover

The Sub-Contractor shall provide written confirmation to the reasonable satisfaction of the Contractor of the existence of the insurance policies as required under this Sub-Contract and that the premium for each policy has been paid. Furthermore the Sub-Contractor shall obtain written confirmation from its insurers that the said insurers will notify the Contractor in the event of any amendment or cancellation of the said insurance policies (including the amount of any excess deductible therein contained).

3(g) Owner Controlled Insurance Programme

If the Works Requirements include provision for an owner controlled insurance programme, the parties hereto shall comply with those provisions and this clause 3 shall be amended, as reasonably required, to give effect to such programme.

NOTE

These are the insurance clauses and are referred to above in Part 1 of the Appendix section C. Clause 3 (e) refers to professional indemnity insurance. This is required for any Sub-Contractor designed works.

4. MANAGEMENT

4(a) Co-operation

The Contractor and the Sub-Contractor shall provide reciprocal co-operation and support for the Sub-Contract purposes. The provisions of clause 4.1. ("Co-operation") of the Main Contract shall apply as between the Contractor and Sub-Contractor in that regard.

4(b) Instructions

(1) The Contractor may issue instructions to the Sub-Contractor in relation to any matter connected with the Sub-Contract Works (whether or not mentioned elsewhere in the Sub-Contract) at any time up to the date of issue of the Defects Certificate. The Sub-Contractor shall comply with the instructions of the Contractor.

(2) Instructions of the Contractor may vary the Sub-Contract Works (including by adding to, omitting and changing the Sub-Contract Works and imposing, removing and changing restrictions on how they are to be executed).

(3) Instructions by the Contractor shall be given in writing except when there is imminent danger to safety or health or of damage to property, in which case the Contractor may give oral instructions and shall confirm them in writing as soon as is practicable.

4(c) Works Proposals & Required Contractor Submissions

To enable the Contractor fully to meet its obligations under clauses 4.6 ("Works Proposals") and 4.7 ("Required Contractor Submissions") of the Main Contract, the Sub-Contractor shall provide any required documents, information, design data or other data and will take all steps necessary in relation to the Sub-Contract Works. The Sub-Contractor is fully responsible for the accuracy and adequacy of its own design (if any) and fully indemnifies the Contractor for any loss sustained by it by reason of any defect in the design of the Sub-Contract Works undertaken by the Sub-Contractor.

4(d)   Programme & Progress Reports

(1)   The Sub-Contractor shall carry out and complete the Sub-Contract Works to meet the requirements of the Main Contract programme in compliance with sub-clause 4(d)(5) hereof.

(2)   The Sub-Contractor shall liaise and cooperate with the Contractor and other sub-contractors of the Contractor and / or other contractors of the Employer engaged on or in connection with the Works and shall so programme and order the Sub-Contract Works so that the Contractor and / or its Sub-Contractors and / or other contractors of the Employer are not delayed or disrupted.

(3)   The Contractor shall give reasonable notice of any information it requires from the Sub-Contractor in respect of programming and progress of the Sub-Contract Works to enable the Contractor to meet its obligations under the Main Contract, including those set out at clauses 4.9 ("Programme") and 4.10 ("Progress Reports") and the Sub-Contractor shall provide the required information in such detail and in such time as will enable the Contractor to avoid being in breach of its obligations under the Main Contract.

(4)   If required by the Contractor, the Sub-Contractor shall provide information for the Contractor's programme including the details of the following:-

 (i)   when the Sub-Contractor will require any instructions, Works Items or any other things to be given by the Employer or the Contractor

 (ii)   a programme showing the order in which the Subcontractor proposes to execute the Sub-Contract Works and the duration of the various Sub-Contract activities

 (iii)   Details of procurement, manufacture, delivery, construction, testing and commissioning of the Sub-Contract Works Items and the sequence and timing of inspections and tests.

 (iv)   Where the Main Contract is a public works contract for civil engineering works, the methods by which the Sub-Contractor proposes to execute the Sub-Contract Works and any temporary works.

(5)   (i)   The Sub-Contractor's programme shall allow reasonable periods of time for the Employer, the Employer's Personnel or the Contractor to comply with their respective obligations under the Main Contract and under the Sub-Contract

 (ii)   The Sub-Contractor's programme shall comply with the Contractor's programme at all times and shall be revised from time to time, as necessary, to do so. The Contractor shall not revise its programme unreasonably or to an unreasonable extent.

 (iii)   If at any time the Sub-Contractor's then applicable programme does not comply with the actual progress of the Sub-Contract Works or with the Sub-Contractor's obligations or the Contractor's obligations, the Sub-Contractor, if so directed by the Contractor, shall submit a revised programme which complies with this Sub-Contract and reflects the actual progress position at that time.

(6)   The Sub-Contractor shall provide to the Contractor monthly progress reports from the commencement of the Sub-Contract Works until the completion thereof. The first report shall relate to the period from the commencement date up to the end of the month in which it occurs and each subsequent report shall relate to each subsequent month. The Sub-Contractor shall provide each progress report within four working days after the end of the month to which it relates. Each progress report shall be in the format required by the Contractor to meet its obligations under the Main Contract.

(7)   Each progress report shall include in relation to the Sub-Contract Works such detail as is reasonably required by the Contractor to meet its obligations under clause 4.10 ("Progress Reports"),

sub-clause 4.10.2 of the Main Contract and shall include, unless the Sub-Contractor is informed otherwise in writing, the following:-

   (i)   a detailed description of progress of each stage of the Sub-Contract Works

   (ii)   the names of off-site suppliers in relation to the Sub-Contract Works, and the progress and location of the design, manufacture, fabrication, delivery, installation, testing and commissioning of Sub-Contract Works Items

   (iii)   details of the Sub-Contractor's Personnel and Sub-Contractor's Things on the Site

   (iv)   status of preparation and review of Sub-Contract Documents

   (v)   copies of quality assurance documents and tests results and certificates

   (vi)   details of when any instructions to be provided by the Contractor or by the Employer's Representative will be required, and any that are outstanding

   (vii)   details of when any Sub-Contract Works Items or other things to be provided by the Employer or the Contractor will be required and any that are outstanding

   (viii)   details of any Delay Events and Compensation Events relating to the Sub-Contract Works that have occurred during the period, or are unresolved

   (ix)   details of any accidents, injuries, hazardous incidents, environmental incidents, labour relations problems and public relations problems arising in relation to or affecting the Sub-Contract Works

   (x)   details of anything that might have an adverse effect on the execution of the Sub-Contract Works, the steps the Sub-Contractor is taking or proposed to take to reduce those risks, and any steps that the Sub-Contractor proposes that the Contractor or Employer should take to reduce those risks

   (xi)   anything else that the Sub-Contractor considers relevant to a progress report

   (xii)   anything else relevant to a progress report that the Contractor reasonably directs.

(8)   If, provided reasonable notice has been given by the Contractor of the requirement for programme or progress report information, due to the Sub-Contractor's failure to submit such information to the Contractor in accordance with this clause, the Contractor suffers a payment reduction under clauses 4.9.3 or 11.4.2 of the Main Contract, the Contractor shall, subject to clause 11(b) hereof, be entitled to deduct the same amount from the next payment to the Sub-Contractor. To the extent that the deduction is partially caused by default of the Sub-Contractor, a fair and reasonable proportion of the sum withheld by the Employer shall be withheld from the Sub-Contractor.

NOTE

The Sub-Contractor shall carry out and complete the Sub-Contract works to meet the requirements of the Main Contract programme.

The Sub-Contractor shall liaise and co-operate with the Contractor and other Sub-Contractors and shall programme the Sub-Contract works so that they are not delayed or disrupted.

The Sub-Contractor is required to provide relevant information in respect of programming and progress of the Sub-Contract works to enable the Contractor to meet their obligations under the Main Contract in relation to programme and progress reporting.

The Sub-Contractor must provide information for the Contractor's programme in relation to when they will require any instructions, works items or any other thing to be given by the Employer or the Contractor, a programme showing the order in which they propose to execute the works and the duration of the various activities, details of procurement, manufacture, delivery, construction, testing and commissioning of works items and the sequence and timing of inspections and tests, and for civil engineering works, the methods by which the Sub-Contractor proposes to execute the works and any temporary works.

The Sub-Contractor must co-operate with the Employer, the Employer's personnel or the Contractor in relation to preparation, monitoring and revision of the programme.

The Sub-Contractor must provide monthly progress reports within four working days after the end of the month to which it relates. It shall be in the format required by the Contractor to meet its obligation under the Main Contract. There are 12 headings listed in sub-clause 4(d)(7) which should be included in the progress reports:

  i) a detailed description of progress of each stage of the Sub-Contract Works;

  ii) the names of off-site suppliers in relation to the Sub-Contract Works, and the progress and location of the design, manufacture, fabrication, delivery, installation, testing and commissioning of Sub-Contract Works Items;

  iii) details of the Sub-Contractor's Personnel and Sub-Contractor's Things on the Site;

  iv) status of preparation and review of Sub-Contract Documents;

  v) copies of quality assurance documents and tests results and certificates;

  vi) details of when any instructions to be provided by the Contractor or by the Employer's Representative will be required, and any that are outstanding;

  vii) details of when any Sub-Contract Works Items or other things to be provided by the Employer or the Contractor will be required and any that are outstanding;

  viii) details of any Delay Events and Compensation Events relating to the Sub-Contract Works that have occurred during the period, or are unresolved;

  ix) details of any accidents, injuries, hazardous incidents, environmental incidents, labour relations problems and public relations problems arising in relation to or affecting the Sub-Contract Works;

  x) details of anything that might have an adverse effect on the execution of the Sub-Contract Works, the steps the Sub-Contractor is taking or proposed to take to reduce those risks, and any steps that the Sub-Contractor proposes that the Contractor or Employer should take to reduce those risks;

  xi) anything else that the Sub-Contractor considers relevant to a progress report;

  xii) anything else relevant to a progress report that the Contractor reasonably directs.

Under the Main Contract if the Contractor fails to provide a revised programme within 15 working days of a request from when the Employer's Representative, then the Employer may deduct 15 percent of any payment due to the Contractor until the new programme is provided. Clause 4(d)(8) of the Sub-Contract allows the main Contractor to pass on this penalty to the Sub-Contractor to the extent that the deduction is partially caused by default of the Sub-Contractor.

4(e)   Notice and Time for Contractors Obligations

(1) The Sub-Contractor shall give the Contractor at least 12 working days advance notice of the date by which the Sub-Contractor requires any instructions or any other thing that the Contractor is to provide.

(2) To the extent that the Sub-Contractor requires any instructions or other thing from the Contractor to enable it proceed with the Sub-Contract Works, the same will be provided by the Contractor within a reasonable time. However, to the extent that such instructions or other thing are to be provided by the Employer or Employer's Representative to the Contractor

under the Main Contractor, the Contractor's only obligation to the Sub-Contractor will be to pass on such instructions or other thing to the Sub-Contractor within a reasonable time of receipt from the Employer or the Employer's Representative.

NOTE

The Sub-Contractor must provide 12 working days advance notice of the date by which instructions or work items or other things are required from the Contractor. This can be carried out when producing the programme and a full list provided to the Contractor when providing the programme. Any failure by the Contractor to provide the requested information on time will entitle the Sub-Contractor to an extension of time and costs arising from resultant delays.

4(f)   Meetings

The Sub-Contractor shall attend meetings with the Contractor and with the Employer's Representative or other relevant parties at such times and venues as the Contractor may reasonably require. If the Sub-Contractor is provided with minutes of any such meeting, the Sub-Contractor shall notify the Contractor of any objection to the minutes within 3 working days of receipt. Otherwise, unless clearly wrong, the minutes shall be considered correct.

NOTE

Regular meetings shall take place which the Sub-Contractor will be required to attend.

4(g)   Proposed Instructions

If any request is made by the Employer's Representative under clause 10.4 ("Proposed Instructions") of the Main Contract for proposals for a Proposed Instruction, the Sub-Contractor shall provide such calculations and information (including design details if appropriate) as is necessary for the Contractor to comply with that request in so far as the request relates to the Sub-Contract Works and will do so in sufficient time to enable the Contractor meet the time requirements of that provision.

NOTE

Under the Main Contract the Contractor is required to submit proposed instructions that may be requested from the Employer's representative. The Sub-Contractor must provide information as is necessary for the Contractor to comply with the request in so far as the request relates to the Sub-Contract Works and will do so in sufficient time.

4(h)   Sub-Contractor's Things not to be removed

The Sub-Contractor shall submit details to the Contractor before removing any Sub-Contractor's Things from the Site prior to the issue by the Employer's Representative of the Certificate of Substantial Completion of the whole of the Works or of a Section of the Works.

NOTE

The Sub-Contractor must inform the Contractor before he removes any Sub-Contractor's things from site before substantial completion.

5. SUB-CONTRACTOR'S PERSONNEL

> **NOTE**
> This clause deals with Liability, Qualifications and Competence.

5(a) Liability

The Sub-Contractor is liable for the acts and omissions of Sub-Contractor Personnel [including any design carried out] as if they were the Sub-Contractor's own acts and omissions.

5(b) Qualifications and Competence

The Sub-Contractor shall ensure that the Sub-Contractor Personnel are suitably qualified and experienced and competent to carry out their respective tasks.

5(c) Pay and Conditions of Employment of Sub-Contractor's Personnel

(1) The provisions of clause 5.3 ("Pay and Conditions of Employment") of the Main Contract will apply, *mutatis mutandis,* to the Sub-Contractor in respect of the Sub-Contractor's Personnel.

(2) Sub-clause 5.3.3A(2) of the Main Contract shall only be included as a term of the Sub-Contract if the Schedule to the Main Contract Part 1J says so, and if not, neither sub-clause 5.3.3A(2) nor its omission shall be taken into account. In the event of 5.3.3A(2) applying, the Sub-Contractor will grant to the Employer and to the Contractor every facility and co-operation and will ensure that the Sub-Contractor's Personnel does likewise in that regard.

(3) If the Sub-Contractor has not complied with this clause 5(c), the Contractor shall (without limiting its other rights or remedies) be entitled to estimate the amount that should have been paid to work persons (and contributions that should have been made on their behalf), and the Contractor may deduct the estimated amount from any payment due to the Sub-Contractor, until the Contractor is satisfied that all proper amounts have been paid.

(4) The Sub-Contractor shall give to the Contractor with each Sub-Contractor's Interim Statement under clause 11(a), a certificate in respect of the work to which the Interim Statement relates to the effect that the Sub-Contractor and the Sub-Contractor's Personnel have complied in full with this clause 5(c). The certificate will be in similar form to that required of the Contractor under the terms of the Main Contract subject to such modifications as the Contractor may reasonably require.

> **NOTE**
> Under the Main Contract the Contractor shall ensure that the rates of pay and conditions of employment of each work person comply with the applicable law and are no less favourable than those for the relevant category of work person in any employment agreement registered under the Industrial relations Acts 1946–2004. Under sub-clause 5(c) of the Sub-Contact this obligation is passed on to the Sub-Contractor.
>
> Under the Main Contract to confirm compliance with this clause the Contractor has to provide the Employer's Representative with a Certificate – Model Form 15 – that the Contractor has complied in full with clause 5.3. The Contractor has to submit this certificate with each interim statement under clause 11.1 (Interim Payment) otherwise payment will be delayed. This requirement is passed on to the Sub-Contractor in the sub-contract.

5(d) Sub-Sub-Contractors

The Sub-Contractor shall not subcontract the Sub-Contract Works, in whole or in part, without the consent in writing of the Contractor.

5(e) Collateral Warranties

If the Appendix Part 1 states that a collateral warranty is required from the Sub-Contractor, the Sub-Contractor shall provide to the Contractor a collateral warranty in the form included in the Works Requirements (or if there is none a form approved by the Employer) executed by the Sub-Contractor on or before the date it is required under the terms of the Main Contract. If the Employer makes any deduction from payments otherwise due to the Contractor under the terms of the Main Contract because any such collateral warranty has not been provided, the Contractor will be entitled, subject to clause 11(b) hereof, to withhold payment of the sum specified in the Main Contract Schedule Part 1 F from any sum due to the Sub-Contractor until the collateral warranty is provided.

5(f) Removal of Work Persons

The Sub-Contractor shall remove from the site any Sub-Contractor Personnel where the Employer's Representative so directs under the terms of the Main Contract. The Sub-Contractor will also remove from the site any Sub-Contractor Personnel where the Contractor so directs because of the Sub-Contractor Personnel's negligence or incompetence or on the basis that the Sub-Contractor Personnel's presence on the site is not conducive to safety, health or good order.

6. PROPERTY

6(a) Ownership of Work Items and Infringement of Property Rights

The Sub-Contractor will ensure that in so far as sub-clauses 6.1 and 6.2 of the Main Contract relate to Sub-Contract Works Items, Sub-Contractor Things or otherwise relate to the Sub-Contract Works, that the Contractor is not in breach of those provisions.

> **NOTE**
>
> "Work items" mean a part of the Sub-Contract Works, or anything that the Sub-Contractor intends will become part of the Works and Temporary Works for the Works.

6(b) Works Requirements

The Works Requirements shall remain the property of the Employer and the Sub-Contractor shall not use them (and shall ensure that the Sub-Contractor's Personnel do not use them) for any purpose other than to perform the Sub-Contract or to prosecute or defend a dispute under the Sub-Contract.

6(c) Property and Rights in Sub-Contractor's Documents

The entitlements of the Employer in relation to the Contractor's Documents under clause 6.4 of the Main Contract will apply in relation to the Sub-Contract Documents and the obligations of the Contractor under that clause will apply *mutatis mutandis* to the Sub-Contractor in relation to the Sub-Contractor's Documents.

> **NOTE**
>
> Under the Main Contract the Employer can request ownership in relation to the Contractor's documents. This will apply to Sub-Contractor's documents and the obligations of the Contractor under that clause will apply equally to the Sub-Contractor in relation to the sub-contract's documents.

7. THE SITE

7(a) Lands Made Available for the Works

Subject to any restrictions in the Works Requirements, the Contractor shall from time to time make available to the Sub-Contractor such part or parts of the Site and such means of access thereto within the Site as shall be necessary to enable the Sub-Contractor to execute the Sub-Contract Works in accordance with the Sub-Contract, but the Contractor shall not be bound to give the Sub-Contractor exclusive possession or exclusive control of any part of the Site, save as expressly provided for otherwise in the Sub-Contract Documents.

> **NOTE**
>
> The Contractor shall, from time to time, make available to the Sub-Contractor such part or parts of the site and such means of access thereto within the site as shall be necessary to enable the Sub-Contractor to execute the sub-contract works in accordance with the sub-contract, but the Contractor shall not be bound to give the Sub-Contractor exclusive possession or exclusive control of any part of the site, save as expressly provided for otherwise in the sub-contract documents.

7(b) Scaffolding

The Contractor shall permit the Sub-Contractor for the purpose of executing and completing the Sub-Contract Works to use such standing scaffolding as is from time to time provided by the Contractor in connection with the Works, but the Contractor shall not be bound to provide or retain such scaffolding for the Sub-Contractor's use unless otherwise stated in the Sub-Contract Documents.

7(c) Attendances

(1) The Contractor shall provide general attendances as stated in the Method of Measurement identified in the Appendix Part 1. Special attendances listed in the Appendix Part 1 will be provided by the Contractor. Otherwise the Sub-Contractor shall provide everything necessary for the execution of the Sub-Contract Works. The Contractor will provide all attendances required by this clause in a timely manner so as not to cause delay or disrupt progress of the Sub-Contract Works.

(2) The Sub-Contractor will be responsible for and bear the cost (to the extent that this cost is not recoverable as Compensation Event under the Main Contract) of removal from site and disposal of hazardous waste (as defined by Section 4(2)(a) of the Waste Act 1996) arising from the execution of the Sub-Contract Works.

7(d) Security and Safety of the Site and Nuisance

The Sub-Contractor will ensure that neither it nor the Sub-Contractor Personnel will cause the Contractor to be in breach of clause 7.5 ("Security and Safety of the Site and Nuisance") of the Main Contract.

7(e) Access and Traffic Control

The Sub-Contractor shall provide at its own cost for any necessary traffic control and access to the Sub-Contract Works, and shall take all reasonable steps to ensure that its traffic and that of the Sub-Contractor Personnel:-

(i) complies with the restrictions concerning laden weight and dimensions in the Law; and

(ii) does not damage roads (except for ordinary wear) bridges or other property.

7(f)   Setting Out The Works

Unless otherwise agreed between the parties, the Sub-Contractor will set out the Sub-Contract Works in compliance with clause 7.7 ("Setting Out the Works") of the Main Contract.

7(g)   Archaeological Objects and Human Remains

If any fossils, coins, antiquities, monuments or other items of value or of archaeological or geological interest or human remains are discovered on or adjacent to the Site, the Sub-Contractor shall not disturb them, but shall take all necessary steps to preserve them, and shall promptly notify the Contractor and comply with any instructions. As between the parties, these items shall be the Contractor's property.

7(h)   Condition of Site on Completion

At Substantial Completion of the Works or of any Section of the Works, of which the Sub-Contract Works form the whole or part, the Sub-Contractor shall remove from the Site (or section of the Site, as the case may be) the Sub-Contractor's Things not required to perform the Sub-Contractor's remaining obligations, and leave the Works or Section in an orderly manner. At the end of the Defects Period, the Sub-Contractor shall remove from the Site any remaining Sub-Contractor's Things.

7(i)   Working Times

The Sub-Contractor shall ensure that the Sub-Contractor's Personnel work on the Site only during the working times permitted under the terms of the Main Contract unless:-

(i)   there is imminent danger to safety or health or of damage to the Works or other property or

(ii) otherwise agreed with the Contractor.

8. QUALITY, TESTING AND DEFECTS

8(a) Standards of Workmanship and Works Items

The Sub-Contractor shall ensure all of the following:-

(1) that the Sub-Contract Works are designed (to the extent that this is the Sub-Contractor's responsibility), executed and completed:

   (i) in accordance with all the requirements in, and reasonably inferred from, the Main Contract, the Contractor's Documents, the Sub-Contract and the Sub-Contractor's Documents.

   (ii) In a proper and workmanlike manner and using good practice.

(2) that all Sub-Contract Works Items (whether or not the Sub-Contractor is required to select them):-

   (i) comply with the Sub-Contract and the Legal Requirements

   (ii) are (unless the Sub-Contract provides otherwise) new and of good quality

(3) that all materials and goods that are Sub-Contract Works Items are fit for their intended purpose in the Works

(4) that the completed Sub-Contract Works are fit for their intended purpose as stated in or to be inferred from the Works Requirements or from the Sub-Contract.

8(b) Quality Assurance

The Sub-Contractor shall establish and implement quality assurance procedures as required by the Main Contract Works Requirements in so far as they relate to the Sub-Contract Works, including procedures for establishing quality assurance systems for itself and any sub-sub-contractors. The quality assurance procedures shall be reflected in appropriate quality plans submitted to the Contractor. The Sub-Contractor shall give to the Contractor copies of all reports prepared in accordance with the Sub-Contractor quality assurance procedures. The Employer's Representative or the Contractor may monitor, spot check and audit the Sub-Contractor's quality assurance procedures and the Sub-Contractor will cooperate with the Employer's Representative and with the Contractor in the conduct of any such spot check.

> **NOTE**
>
> The Sub-Contractor shall establish and implement quality assurance requirements as required by the Main Contract Works requirements in so far as they relate to the sub-contract works, including procedures for establishing quality assurance systems for itself and any sub Sub-Contractors. The quality assurance procedures shall be reflected in appropriate quality plans that the Sub-Contractor submits to the Contractor. The quality assurance procedures shall be reflected in appropriate quality plans that the Contractor submits to the Employer's representative. The Employer's representative or the Contractor may monitor, carry out spot checks and audit the Sub-Contractor's quality assurance procedures.

8(c) Inspection and Tests

(1) The Sub-Contractor will have the same rights and obligations in relation to the Sub-Contract Works, *mutatis mutandis*, as the Contractor has under clause 8.3 ("Inspection") of the Main Contract in relation to the Works.

(2) The Sub-Contractor will have the same rights and obligations in relation to the Sub-Contract Works, *mutatis mutandis*, as the Contractor has under clause 8.4 ("Tests") of the Main Contract in relation to the Works. The Employer's Representative, others authorised by the Employer and the Contractor may attend and observe the tests and the Sub-Contractor shall facilitate such attendance and observation.

8(d) Defects

(1) The Contractor may direct the Sub-Contractor to search for a Defect or suspected Defect or its cause. This may include uncovering, dismantling, re-covering and re-erecting work, providing facilities for tests, testing and inspecting. If, through searching or otherwise, the Sub-Contractor discovers a Defect, the Sub-Contractor shall notify the Contractor as soon as practicable.

(2) If, through notification or otherwise, the Contractor becomes aware of a Defect, the Contractor may direct the Sub-Contractor to do any or all of the following:-

   (i)   to remove the defective Sub-Contract Works Item from the Site

   (ii) to demolish the defective Sub-Contract Works Item, if incorporated in the Works.

   (iii) to reconstruct, replace or correct the defective Sub-Contract Works Item

   (iv) not to deliver the defective Sub-Contract Works Item to the Site

(3) The Sub-Contractor shall comply with any direction under this sub-clause 8(d) within the reasonable times (if any) the Contractor directs and in any event within any time limit imposed by the Employer's Representative. If the Sub-Contractor fails to begin the work required to comply with the direction within the reasonable time directed (if any) or fails to complete it as soon as practicable, the Contractor may have the work done by others and the Sub-Contractor shall on request pay the Contractor the cost thereby incurred.

(4) Alternatively, the Contractor and the Employer's Representative may, with the Employer's and Sub-Contractor's agreement, agree that the Employer will accept the Defect, either in whole or subject to any change to the Works Requirements that the Employer's Representative directs. In this case, the Sub-Contract Sum shall be reduced by the amount that, in the opinion of the Employer's Representative, is the resulting decrease in the value of the Works to the Employer. If the Contractor notifies the Sub-Contractor that the Employer will not accept a Defect, this shall be conclusive. Notwithstanding this provision, the Sub-Contractor shall be entitled in any case to make good any Defect in the Sub-Contract Works and thus avoid a deduction from the Sub-Contract Sum in respect of the Defect.

(5) If a Defect in the Sub-Contract Works deprives the Employer of substantially the whole benefit of the Works or any Section or other material part of the Works, the Employer's Representative may reject the Works or the relevant part of the Works. In this event, the Sub-Contractor will indemnify the Contractor in relation to any loss incurred by the Contractor under clause 8.5 ("Defects") of the Main Contract or otherwise.

8(e) Defects Period & Defects Certificate

(1) As soon as practicable, the Sub-Contractor shall complete any outstanding works and rectify any Defects brought to his attention by the Contractor either prior to Substantial Completion or during the Defects Period. In so doing, and in conducting any tests after Substantial Completion, the Sub-Contractor shall cause as little disruption as possible to occupants and users of the Works.

(2) The Sub-Contractor will indemnify the Contractor in relation to any reduction to the Contract Sum made under clause 8.5 ("Defects") of the Main Contract in so far as that reduction relates to a Defect in the Sub-Contract Works.

(3) Nothing in this clause nor any exercise or non-exercise by the Employer, the Employer's Representative or the Contractor of their rights under this clause 8(e), nor the Defects Certificate, relieves the Sub-Contractor of any obligation in relation to any Defect in the Sub-Contract Works, except to the extent that a Defect is accepted by agreement under sub-clause 8(d)(4) hereof.

9. TIME AND COMPLETION

9(a) Starting Date

The Sub-Contractor shall commence work on site within ten working days, or such other period as may be entered in the Appendix Part 1, of receipt of the Contractor's written instructions so to do and shall thereafter proceed with due diligence with the execution and completion of the Sub-Contract Works. The Contractor shall ensure that the Sub-Contractor has sufficient information to enable it to commence the Sub-Contract Works and to proceed with them diligently.

9(b) Suspension

(1) The Contractor may instruct the Sub-Contractor to suspend all or part of the Sub-Contract Works if the Contractor has been instructed to suspend work by the Employer / Employer's Representative or the Contractor has suspended the Works by reason of not being paid by the Employer. The Sub-Contractor shall comply with the instruction and, during the suspension, shall protect, store and secure the affected Sub-Contract Works Items against deterioration, loss and damage and maintain the Sub-Contract Insurances. The Sub-Contractor shall take all reasonable steps to mitigate any loss suffered as a consequence of the suspension.

(2) The Contractor will have no liability to the Sub-Contractor for any loss or delay suffered by the Sub-Contractor by reason of any such suspension except to the extent that the Contractor actually recovers payment from the Employer in relation thereto. If payment is made by the Employer to the Contractor in relation to losses sustained by reason of such suspension the Sub-Contractor will be entitled to such proportion thereof as is fair and reasonable in all the circumstances.

> **NOTE**
>
> The Contractor may request the Sub-Contractor to suspend the works. In the event of a suspension the works have to be protected, stored and kept secure. The works will be resumed on instruction from the Contractor. The Sub-Contractor is entitled to the cost of any remedial works. The Sub-Contractor is entitled to an adjustment of the sub-contract sum and an extension of time, both of which have to be assessed.

9(c) Notification of Delay

If the Sub-Contractor becomes aware or should have become aware that the Sub-Contract Works are being or are likely to be delayed for any reason, it shall notify the Contractor of the delay and its cause as soon as practicable but in any event within ten working days. Within a further 20 working days the Sub-Contractor shall give the Contractor full details of the delay in writing and its effect on the progress of the Sub-Contract Works. The Sub-Contractor will promptly provide any further information in relation to the delay which either the Contractor or the Employer's Representative requests.

> **NOTE**
>
> The Sub-Contractor shall as soon as he becomes aware, or should have become aware that the sub-contract works are being or are likely to be delayed, he must notify the Contractor of the delay and the cause, as soon as practicable, but in any event within 10 working days. Within a further 20 working days the Sub-Contractor shall provide full details of the delay and the effect on progress of the works. The Sub-Contractor shall promptly provide any further information in relation to the delay as may be requested by the Contractor or the Employer's representative. So notice of delays can be time-barred if they are not issued within the stated period.
>
> The time restraints, i.e., 10 working days after the Sub-Contractor became aware of the delay and a further 20 working days to provide full details, must be strictly adhered to.

9(d) Programme Contingency

The Sub-Contractor has not included in the initial Sub-Contract Sum for unrecovered costs caused by Compensation Events. No deductions on account of the Programme Contingency provisions in the Main Contract therefore will be made from any delay costs to which the Sub-Contractor may be entitled.

NOTE

The rigid procedures applicable to programme contingencies as contained in the Main Contract clause 9.4 are not applicable to the domestic sub-contract. They do, however, apply to the NN sub-contract.

10. CLAIMS AND ADJUSTMENTS

10(a) Notification and Procedure

(1) If the Sub-Contractor considers that it is entitled to an adjustment to the Sub-Contract Sum or that it has any other entitlement under or in relation to the Sub-Contract (including damages for breach of contract on the part of the Contractor), the Sub-Contractor shall, as soon as practicable and in any event within 10 working days after it became aware or should have become aware of such entitlement, give notice of this to the Contractor. The notice must prominently state that it is being given under this sub-clause 10(a)(1). Within a further 20 working days after giving the notice, the Sub-Contractor will give to the Contractor details of the following:-

   (i) all relevant facts about the claim

   (ii) a detailed calculation and (so far as practicable) a proposal, based on that calculation, of any adjustment to be made to the Sub-Contract Sum and of the amount of any other entitlement claimed by the Sub-Contractor

   (iii) if the total number of Site Working Days required for completion of the Sub-Contract works is increased by the delay, full details of the extent of the delay and the effect it is likely to have on the completion of the Sub-Contract works.

(2) The Sub-Contractor shall provide any further information requested by the Contractor in relation to the event or circumstance.

(3) If the Sub-Contractor does not give notice and details in accordance with and within the time provided in sub-clause 10(a)(1) notwithstanding anything else in the Sub-Contract the Sub-Contractor shall not be entitled to an increase to the Sub-Contract Sum and the Contractor shall be released from all liability to the Sub-Contractor in relation to the matter, except to the extent that the Contractor recovers additional payment from the Employer in respect of the Sub-Contract Works notwithstanding the failure of the Sub-Contractor to give such notice, in which case the Sub-Contractor will be entitled to corresponding payment valued in accordance with the Sub-Contract.

(4) If the cause of the claim has a continuing effect, the Sub-Contractor shall update the above information at monthly intervals.

(5) The Sub-Contractor shall keep detailed contemporary records to substantiate any aspect of an event or circumstance in relation to which it has, or is entitled to, give notice under this sub-clause 10(a) and its resulting costs. These shall include any records the Contractor directs the Sub-Contractor to keep. The Sub-Contractor shall provide the records to the Contractor if so directed.

NOTE

If the Sub-Contractor considers that there should be an extension of time or an adjustment to the contract sum he shall provide such notice to the Contractor within 10 working days after becoming or should have been aware of something that would give rise to an entitlement. The notice must prominently state that it is being given under sub-clause 10(a)(1).

Within a further 20 working days after giving the notice, the Sub- Contractor shall provide:

   i) All relevant facts;

   ii) A detailed calculation and a proposal based on the calculation of the adjustment to be made to the contract sum and of the amount of any other entitlement claimed by the Sub-Contractor.

The Sub-Contractor shall provide any further information requested by the Contractor in relation to the matter.

If the Sub-Contractor does not comply with notices, details and time scales, then the Sub-Contractor shall not be entitled to an increase in the contract sum and the Contractor shall be released from all liability to the Sub-Contractor in relation to the matter except to the extent that the Contractor recovers additional payment from the Employer in respect of the sub-contract works. Sub-clause 10(5) requires the Sub-Contractor to keep contemporary records of all events under 10(a). The Contractor may instruct the Sub-Contractor to keep records.

This requirement places pressure on the Contractor's management and surveying staff to ensure the Contractor's entitlements are not in any way compromised. Therefore, sufficient staff will have to be allocated to the project.

10(b)   Adjustments to the Sub-Contract Sum

(1)   Adjustments to the Sub-Contract Sum may arise in respect of additional work, substituted work or omitted work as a consequence of a Compensation Event (as defined in the Schedule Part 1 K of the Main Contract and provided it is not a Sub-Contractor's Risk Event), or as a consequence of a Contractor's Risk Event (listed in Section I of the Appendix Part 1) or as a consequence of complying with an instruction from the Contractor in relation to a matter which could not reasonably have been anticipated by the Sub-Contractor at the time of tendering.

(2)   If the additional work, substituted work or omitted work is the same as or similar to work for which there are rates in the Sub-Contractor's tender and is to be executed under similar conditions, the adjustment of the Sub-Contract Sum shall be determined using those rates.

(3)   If the additional work, substituted work or omitted work is not similar to work for which there are rates in the Sub-Contractor's tender and is not to be executed under similar conditions, the adjustment of the Sub-Contract Sum shall be determined on the basis of the rates in the Sub-Contractor's tender when that is reasonable.

(4)   If the adjustment can not be determined under the above rules, the Contractor shall make a fair valuation.

(5)   The Contractor may direct that adjustment to the Sub-Contract Sum in respect of additional work or substituted work will be determined on the basis of the cost of performing the additional or substituted work, compared with the Sub-Contractor's cost without the Compensation Event, Contractor's instruction or Contractor's Risk Event (as the case may be), as follows:-

(i)   The number of hours worked or to be worked by each category of work person stated in the Appendix Part 2 and engaged on the work to which the Compensation Event or Contractor's Instruction (as the case may be) relates, on or off the Site, multiplied in each case by the tendered hourly rate for that category stated in the Appendix Part 2.

(ii)   The cost of materials used in that work, taking into account discounts and excluding VAT, plus the percentage adjustment tendered by the Sub-Contractor and stated in the Appendix Part 2.

(iii)   The cost of plant reasonably used for that work whether hired or owned by the Sub-Contractor, at the rates in the document listed in the Schedule Part 1 K of the Main Contract plus or minus the percentage adjustment tendered by the Sub-Contractor and stated in the Appendix Part 2. If the document listed in the Schedule to the Main Contract does not give a rate for a plant item, the rate inserted in the Appendix Part 2 shall apply (without adjustment) or, if none, a market rental rate shall be used. If the Contractor is entitled to be paid by the Employer for the cost of plant provided by the Sub-Contractor and the market rental rate applies, the hourly rate shall be the market rental rate plus or minus the percentage adjustment. Otherwise the market rental rate (if applicable) shall not be adjusted.

(iv)   The cost of design (if any) at the tendered rate.

(6) Where the adjustment to the Sub-Contract Sum arises as a consequence of a Compensation Event, the method of its determination shall correspond to that being applied by the Employer's Representative under Clause 10.6 of the Main Contract, unless otherwise agreed between the Contractor and the Sub-Contractor.

(7) Adjustments for delay cost shall be in accordance with sub-clause 10 (c) below.

> **NOTE**
>
> The adjustment to the contract sum for a compensation event follows the traditional contract forms, i.e., using rates contained in the pricing document, fair rates or recorded hours by the rates stated in Appendix, Part 2, together with the cost of plant and materials with the percentage additions quoted in Appendix, Part 2.

10(c) Cost of Delay or Disruption

(1) To the extent that the Sub-Contractor is delayed or incurs loss by reason of a Compensation Event (provided it is not a Sub-Contractor's Risk Event), or as a consequence of a Contractor's Risk Event (listed in Section I of the Appendix Part 1) or as a consequence of complying with an instruction from the Contractor in relation to a matter which could not reasonably have been anticipated by the Sub-Contractor at the time of tendering, subject to clause 10(a) hereof, the Sub-Contractor will be entitled to be compensated.

(2) To the extent that the Sub-Contractor incurs delay or loss by reason of any event other than as provided for in sub-clauses 10(c)(1) or 1(g), the Sub-Contractor will have no entitlement to be compensated.

(3) If a delay has more than one cause, and one or more of the causes is not an event for which there is an entitlement to additional payment or recovery of costs incurred, there shall be no increase to the Sub-Contract Sum in respect of the delay cost for the period of concurrent delay.

(4) To the extent that the Sub-Contractor is entitled to compensation for delay caused by Compensation Events under sub-clause 10(c)(1), there shall be added to the Sub-Contract Sum for each Site Working Day for which compensation is payable either of the following (depending on which option has been selected in the Schedule to the Main Contract Part 1 K):-

   (i)   the daily rate of delay cost tendered by the Sub-Contractor in the Appendix Part 2 hereto, or

   (ii) the expenses (excluding profit and loss of profit) unavoidably incurred by the Sub-Contractor as a result of the delay caused by the Compensation Event.

(5) To the extent that the Sub-Contractor is entitled to compensation for delay due to a cause other than a Compensation Event, the Sub-Contractor is entitled to be reimbursed its reasonable additional costs incurred. However, if the delay has more than one cause which would give rise to an entitlement to compensation and one of the causes is a Compensation Event, compensation shall be in accordance with sub-clause 10(c)(4).

(6) If the Sub-Contractor incurs a loss, other than a delay loss, such that the Sub-Contractor is entitled to be compensated under either of sub-clauses 10(c)(1) or 1(g) the Sub-Contractor is entitled to be reimbursed its reasonable additional costs incurred. If, however, the loss is solely as a consequence of a Compensation Event (which is not a Sub-Contractor's Risk Event), the Sub-Contractor's entitlement to compensation and its quantum shall be determined in accordance with the principles which apply under the Main Contract (disregarding the Programme Contingency provisions).

NOTE

To the extent that the Sub-Contractor is delayed or incurs loss by reason of a compensation event, the Sub-Contractor will be entitled to be compensated.

If the Contractor causes delay or additional cost to the Sub-Contractor, under 10(b), the Sub-Contractor will be entitled to be compensated by the Contractor for the reasonable loss incurred. Delay costs are added as defined in Appendix, Part 2. All the costs are capped to that stated in the Appendix except for damages under 1(g).

10(d) Price Variation

In the event that there is no price fluctuation provision in the Appendix Part 1 H, the Sub-Contract Sum is fixed. If the Appendix provides that the Sub-Contractor is to be compensated for fluctuation in cost, such compensation shall only be to the extent that it is provided for in the Appendix. However, irrespective of the price fluctuation provisions which may be defined in the Appendix, the Sub-Contract Sum will be adjustable in respect of Change in Law in accordance with PV1.1.4 or PV2.4 in the Main Contract, whichever may be applicable.

NOTE

Whichever of clauses PV1 or PV2 has been selected in the Schedule Part 1 M of the Main Contract shall apply to the sub-contract equally.

11. PAYMENT

11(a) Interim Statements

(1) The Contractor shall advise the Sub-Contractor of dates on which it will submit Contractor's Interim Statements in accordance with clause 11.1 ("Interim Payment") of the Main Contract.

(2) Not later than 7 working days before each date for submission of a Contractor's Interim Statement, the Sub-Contractor shall submit to the Contractor a statement (the **Sub-Contractor's Interim Statement**) including a detailed breakdown of the sum it considers to be the value of the Sub-Contract Works completed up to the end of that period and indicating the amount it considers payable in respect of that period, which amount will be calculated as follows:-

   (i)   the cumulative value of the Sub-Contract Works properly designed (to the extent that this is the Sub-Contractor's responsibility) and executed, valued in accordance with the rates and prices used in the calculation of the Sub-Contract Sum, plus

   (ii)   where the Sub-Contractor is required to carry out design of the Sub-Contract Works, the value of design completed to date, plus

   (iii) if applicable [as provided for below in sub-clause 11(e)] the value of unfixed Sub-Contract Works Items, plus

   (iv)   amounts due by the Contractor in respect of Compensation Events under the Main Contract as provided for in clause 10 hereof, plus

   (v)   other sums claimed by the Sub-Contractor in accordance with clause 10 hereof, plus

   (vi)   Other adjustments in accordance with Clause 10 hereof, plus

   (vii) If applicable, any sum payable in relation to price variation under clause 10(d) hereof, less

   (viii) retention in accordance with this clause, less

   (ix)   the total amount of previous payments

(3) The Sub-Contractor's Interim Statements shall be accompanied by sufficient information in relation to progress of the Sub-Contract Works, together with any other supporting evidence required by the Employer's Representative (of which the Contractor will give reasonable notice to the Sub-Contractor), to enable the Contractor to meet the requirements of clause 11.1 ("Interim Payment") of the Main Contract.

(4) The Sub-Contractor will provide with each of the Sub-Contractor's Interim Statements the certificate required by clause 5(c)(4) (Pay and Conditions of Employment of Sub-Contractor's Personnel) hereof. The provision of this certificate is a condition precedent to payment by the Contractor to the Sub-Contractor in respect of that period.

(5) If the Sub-Contractor fails to submit an Interim Statement as and at the time required, the Contractor may include in its Interim Statement its own estimate of the sum due in respect of the Sub-Contract Works but shall not be obliged to do so. In this event, any payment to the Sub-Contractor will be based on that estimate and will be subject to the Sub-Contractor providing an Interim Statement showing that at least this amount is due and providing the certificate (in respect of Pay and Conditions of Employment) required by clause 5(c)(4) hereof.

> ### NOTE
>
> The Contractor shall advise the Sub-Contractor of dates on which it will submit Contractor's Interim Statements in accordance with clause 11.1 ("Interim Payment") of the Main Contract. Not later than seven working days before each date for submission of a Contractor's Interim Statement, the Sub-Contractor shall submit to the Contractor a statement (the Sub-Contractor's Interim Statement)

including a detailed breakdown of the sum it considers to be the value of the Sub-Contract Works completed up to the end of that period and indicating the amount it considers payable in respect of that period, which amount will be calculated as follows:

    (i)   the cumulative value of the Sub-Contract Works properly designed (to the extent that this is the Sub-Contractor's responsibility) and executed, valued in accordance with the rates and prices used in the calculation of the Sub-Contract Sum, plus

    (ii)   the value of design completed to date, plus

    (iii)   the value of unfixed Sub-Contract Works Items, plus

    (iv)   amounts due by the Contractor in respect of Compensation Events under the Main Contract as provided for in clause 10 hereof, plus

    (v)   other sums claimed by the Sub-Contractor, plus

    (vi)   Other adjustments, plus

    (vii)   any sum payable in relation to price variation under clause 10(d) hereof, less

    (viii)   retention in accordance with this clause, less

    (ix)   the total amount of previous payments

The Sub-Contractor's Interim Statements shall be accompanied by sufficient information in relation to progress of the Sub-Contract Works, together with any other supporting evidence required by the Employer's Representative (of which the Contractor will give reasonable notice to the Sub-Contractor), to enable the Contractor to meet the requirements of clause 11.1 ("Interim Payment") of the Main Contract.

The Sub-Contractor will provide with each of the Sub-Contractor's Interim Statements the certificate required by clause 5(c)(4) (Pay and Conditions of Employment of Sub-Contractor's Personnel). The provision of this certificate is a condition precedent to payment by the Contractor to the Sub-Contractor in respect of that period.

If the Sub-Contractor fails to submit an Interim Statement as and at the time required, the Contractor may include in its Interim Statement its own estimate of the sum due in respect of the Sub-Contract Works, but shall not be obliged to do so. In this event, any payment to the Sub-Contractor will be based on that estimate and will be subject to the Sub-Contractor providing an Interim Statement showing that at least this amount is due and providing the certificate (in respect of Pay and Conditions of Employment) required by clause 5(c)(4).

11(b) Deductions

(1)   The Contractor may make equivalent pro-rata deductions from sums otherwise due to the Sub-Contractor as the Employer may make from sums due to the Contractor under clause 11.4 ("Full Payment") of the Main Contract, to the extent that the Contractor's default arises from a failure on the part of the Sub-Contractor to abide by the terms of this Sub-Contract. The Contractor shall notify the Sub-Contractor of the deduction, on or before the date the Sub-Contractor is due to be paid, giving particulars of how it arises and of its computation.

(2)   If the Employer's Representative in any certificate, issued in accordance with Clause 11.1.3 of the Main Contract, makes a reduction in the quantity of any item which is part of the Sub-Contract Works, the Contractor may make a corresponding reduction in the sum due to the Sub-Contractor, provided the reduction by the Employer's Representative was not caused by the Contractor's negligence or breach of contract. The Contractor shall notify the Sub-Contractor of any such deduction, on or before the date the Sub-Contractor is due to be paid, giving full particulars of how the reduction in the sum due has been calculated.

(3)   If the Employer's Representative in any certificate, issued in accordance with Clause 11.1.3 of the Main Contract, makes a deduction in the sum claimed by the Contractor for the Sub-Contract

Works in respect of any Compensation Event, the Contractor may make a corresponding deduction in the sum due to the Sub-Contractor. The Contractor shall notify the Sub-Contractor of any such deduction, on or before the date the Sub-Contractor is due to be paid, giving full particulars of how the deduction in the sum due has been calculated.

(4) The Contractor may deduct from any sum otherwise due to the Sub-Contractor any sum to which the Contractor is entitled by reason of contra-charge in respect of this Sub-Contract or arising as a consequence of any breach by the Sub-Contractor of the terms of this Sub-Contract. The Contractor shall notify the Sub-Contractor of any deduction [other than deductions covered by sub-clauses 11(b)(1), (2) and (3) above] not later than 20 working days after the date for submission of the Contractor's Interim Statement under clause 11(a)(1) hereof, giving the reasons for it. The Contractor shall reasonably take into account any representations by the Sub-Contractor in respect of any deductions from interim payments.

(5) The Contractor will not be entitled to make any deduction unless the Sub-Contractor has first been notified in accordance with sub-clauses (1), (2), (3) and (4) of this sub-clause.

NOTE

The Contractor may make deductions from sums due to the Sub-Contractor as the Employer may make from sums due to the Contractor under clause 11.4 ("Full Payment") of the Main Contract, to the extent that the Contractor's default arises from a failure on the part of the Sub-Contractor to abide by the terms of this sub-contract. The Contractor shall notify the Sub-Contractor of the deduction.

11(c) Interim Payments

(1) The Contractor shall make each interim payment of the sum due to the Sub-Contractor not later than 20 working days after the issue by the Employer's Representative of each certificate in accordance with Clause 11.1.3 of the Main Contract. If the sum paid by the Contractor to the Sub-Contractor is less than shown on the Sub-Contractor's Interim Statement the Contractor, shall, at the time of making payment, provide to the Sub-Contractor a statement showing how the sum paid has been computed. In the event that the sum properly deductible by the Contractor exceeds the sum which would otherwise be payable to the Sub-Contractor, there shall be a debt due from the Sub-Contractor to the Contractor which shall be payable by the Sub-Contractor within 7 working days of either the date when payment would otherwise have been due to the Sub-Contractor or of the notification by the Contractor of the debt, whichever is the later.

(2) If, due to default by the Contractor, payment to the Sub-Contractor is delayed beyond the time limit in sub-clause 11 (c) (1) above, the Sub-Contractor will be entitled to be paid interest for the period of the delay at the rate applicable under S.I. No.388 of 2002 European Communities (Late Payment in Commercial Transactions) Regulations 2002.

(3) The Contractor shall, on request and without delay, advise the Sub-Contractor (providing substantiating documentation) of the dates when the Contractor's interim statements were actually submitted to the Employer's Representative in accordance with Clause 11.1.1 of the Main Contract and the dates on which the Contractor received certificates (for payment) issued by the Employer's Representative in accordance with Clause 11.1.3 of the Main Contract.

(4) In the event that, because the amount due to the Contractor is less than the minimum stated in the Schedule Part 1 L of the Main Contract, no payment certificate is issued by the Employer's Representative for any particular period, the Contractor shall so advise the Sub-Contractor and shall pay the Sub-Contractor the sum due to it not later than 32 working days after the date the Contractor would otherwise have been due to submit its Interim Statement to the Employer.

NOTE

The Contractor shall make each interim payment of the sum due to the Sub-Contractor not later than 20 working days after the issue by the Employer's Representative of each certificate.

The Contractor shall advise the Sub-Contractor of the dates when the Contractor's interim statements were actually submitted to the Employer's Representative and the dates on which the Contractor received certificates (for payment) issued by the Employer's Representative.

In the event that, because the amount due to the Contractor is less than the minimum stated in the Schedule Part 1 L of the Main Contract, no payment certificate is issued by the Employer's Representative for any particular period, the Contractor shall so advise the Sub-Contractor and shall pay the Sub-Contractor the sum due not later than 32 working days after the date the Contractor would otherwise have been due to submit its Interim Statement to the Employer.

11(d) Enforcement

(1) The Sub-Contractor shall not take steps to enforce payment of any sum due until 30 working days after the issue [or deemed issue under clause 11(d)(3) hereof] by the Employer's Representative of a certificate under Clause 11.1.3 of the Main Contract or, in the event that Clause 11(c)(4) applies, within 50 working days after the due date for submission of the Contractor's Interim Statement under the Main Contract unless:-

   (i) The Sub-Contract is terminated

   (ii) the Contractor has suspended work

   (iii) the Main Contract has been terminated

(2) If any of the above sub-paragraphs (i) to (iii) applies, the Sub-Contractor may suspend work immediately and take action to recover the sum due. Otherwise, if the Sub-Contractor has not received payment of the sum due within the period stipulated in sub-clause 11(d)(1) above, the Sub-Contractor may:-

   (i) notify the Contractor of its intention to suspend the Sub-Contract Works

   (ii) not less than 15 working days later, if payment has still not been received, suspend the Sub-Contract Works

   (iii) if after a further 15 working days payment has still not been received, terminate the Sub-Contract

In the event that the Sub-Contractor justifiably suspends the Sub-Contract Works because of non-payment by the Contractor of monies due, the consequent delay will be deemed to have been caused by the Contractor's breach.

(3) If, after receiving a request from the Sub-Contractor under clause 11(c)(3) hereof, the Contractor fails to furnish information as to whether and when the Employer's Representative has issued a certificate (for payment) in accordance with clause 11.1.3 of the Main Contract, a certificate will be deemed to have been issued 20 working days after the due date for submission of the Contractor's Statement under clause 11.1 of the Main Contract. However the certificate will not be deemed to have been issued if the Contractor establishes to the reasonable satisfaction of the Sub-Contractor that such a certificate has not been issued and that this was not due to default or breach of contract on the part of the Contractor.

NOTE

The Sub-Contractor shall not take steps to enforce payment of any sum due until 30 working days after the issue, or deemed issue, by the Employer's Representative of a certificate under clause 11.1.3 of the Main Contract or, in the event that clause 11(c)(4) applies, within 50 working days after the due date for submission of the Contractor's Interim Statement under the Main Contract unless:

   i) The Sub-Contract is terminated;

   ii) the Contractor has suspended work;

   iii) the Main Contract has been terminated.

If any of the above applies, the Sub-Contractor may suspend work immediately and take action to recover the sum due. Otherwise, if the Sub-Contractor has not received payment of the sum due within the period stipulated above, the Sub-Contractor may:

    i)   notify the Contractor of its intention to suspend the sub-contract works;

    ii) not less than 15 working days later, suspend the sub-contract works;

    iii) if after a further 15 working days, terminate the sub-contract.

11(e)   Payment for Unfixed Works Items

The Sub-Contractor will be entitled to seek payment for unfixed Sub-Contract Work Items if payment for them may be claimed under the Main Contract. Payment will be subject to full compliance by the Sub-Contractor with the provisions of clause 11.2 ("Unfixed Works Items") of the Main Contract and to the title vesting in the Employer to the Sub-Contractor's Unfixed Work Items. The Sub-Contractor's entitlement to payment will be dependent upon the Employer's Representative including for such payment in a certificate for payment issued under the Main Contract. In the case of Work Items not delivered to the site, the Sub-Contractor will provide a bond for the benefit of the Contractor equivalent to that required by the Employer under clause 11.2 (2) (f) of the Main Contract and the Sub-Contractor will also bear the reasonable cost incurred by the Contractor in providing such a bond for the Employer, or if the bond relates only in part to Sub-Contract Work Items, the Sub-Contractor will bear a reasonable proportion of that cost.

NOTE

Under the Main Contract the Contractor can be paid for unfixed work items up to a value of 90 percent provided the contract allows such a provision which will be detailed in Part 1 L of the Schedule, provided:

- they have been completed and they are substantially ready to be incorporated in the works;

- title to them has been vested in the Employer;

- they are stored suitably on site.

These provisions are afforded to the Sub-Contractor under the sub-contract.

Payment for goods not delivered to the site is more difficult to secure, that is:

- They have been completed and they are substantially ready to be incorporated in the works;

- Title to them has been vested in the Employer;

- They are stored suitably and marked to show they are the property of the Employer and that their destination is the site;

- They are clearly identified in a list provided to the Employer's Representative and with documentary evidence that title is vested in the Employer;

- They are insured as required by the contract and will be insured while in transit;

- The Employer is provided with a bond by a surety approved by the Employer's Representative for the amount to be paid.

Such requirements will take a large amount of administration. The cost of the bond may negate any value to the Sub-Contractor.

11(f)   Retention

The Contractor shall be entitled to deduct retention money from sums due as interim payments to the Sub-Contractor in accordance with this clause and such retention money shall be held in trust by the Contractor for the Sub-Contractor. Retention shall be deducted (and released) in accordance with the provisions set out in Section K of the Appendix Part 1. In the event that Section K of the Appendix Part 1 has not been completed, retention deduction and release will be as follows:-

(i)   Retention will be deducted from all interim sums due to the Subcontractor at the rate stated in the Schedule to the Main Contract (Part 1L). 20 working days after the issue by the Employer's Representative of the Certificate of Substantial Completion, half the sum so deducted will be payable to the Sub-Contractor and the remaining half (the second moiety) will be payable 20 working days after the issue by the Employer's Representative of the Defects Certificate. If, within 10 working days of the issue of the Certificate of Substantial Completion of the Works (or another date agreed between the Contractor and the Sub-Contractor) the Sub-Contractor provides to the Contractor a retention bond in or equivalent to the form incorporated in the Main Contract Works Requirements or, if there is none, a form approved by the Contractor (which approval is not to be unreasonably withheld) for the amount of the second moiety of retention and executed by a surety approved by the Contractor (approval not to be unreasonably withheld), the Sub-Contractor shall be entitled to be paid the second moiety.

(ii) If by reason of the Employer's Representative issuing a Certificate of Substantial Completion for a Section of the Works, the Contractor becomes entitled to the release of the retention relating to the Sub-Contract Works earlier than would otherwise be the case, the Contractor shall pay to the Sub-Contractor the sum due by way of released retention in respect of the Sub-Contract within 20 working days of the date of the said Certificate of Substantial Completion.

11(g)   Final Statement

The Sub-Contractor shall submit to the Contractor its Final Statement of all sums due to the Sub-Contractor under the Sub-Contract, computed in the manner prescribed in sub-clause 11(a)(2) hereof, not later than five weeks after the date of the Certificate of Substantial Completion of the Works issued by the Employer's Representative (which date is to be promptly advised to the Sub-Contractor by the Contractor). However, this shall not preclude the Sub-Contractor from submitting its Final Statement at an earlier date if it considers the Sub-Contract Works are complete. If the Sub-Contractor's fails to provide its Final Statement, the Contractor will make its own estimate of the final value of the Sub-Contract Works and the final payment due to the Sub-Contractor will be based on that estimate irrespective of whether the Sub-Contractor considers that estimate was too low.

> **NOTE**
>
> Within five weeks after substantial completion is certified, the Sub-Contractor shall provide a final statement which shall include all money that the Sub-Contractor considers due from the Contractor.

11(h)   Additional Work instructed after Substantial Completion

(1)   If, after the date of Substantial Completion has been certified, the Contractor instructs the Sub-Contractor to carry out additional work, either as a consequence of a Compensation Event under the Main Contract or otherwise, in order to obtain payment for it the Sub-Contractor will submit a supplemental account not later than one month after the end of the Defects Period (defined in the Schedule Part 1I of the Main Contract). Payment for this additional work will be included in the final payment to the Sub-Contractor or, in the event that no other payment is due to the Sub-Contractor, payment for the additional work will be not later than four months after the date of the Defects Certificate issued by the Employer's Representative.

(2)   The Contractor shall have no liability to the Sub-Contractor under or in relation to the Sub-Contract for any matter not detailed in the Sub-Contractor's Final Statement except in respect of additional work arising from an instruction from the Contractor issued after Substantial Completion of the Works was certified.

11(i)   Penultimate Payment

(1)   The Employer's Representative is required, by the Main Contract, to issue the Penultimate Payment Certificate within five months of the date of Substantial Completion of the Works. Unless the Sub-Contractor's final account has been agreed and all payments due under it have been paid by the Contractor at an earlier date, within 20 working days of the issue by the Employer's Representative of the Penultimate Payment Certificate the Contractor shall pay the Sub-Contractor its Penultimate Payment being the sum due in respect of its Final Statement. If this differs from the sum claimed in the Sub-Contractor's Final Statement, the Contractor shall notify the Sub-Contractor of the differences and of the reasons for them.

(2)   At the time of the Penultimate Payment, if there are deductions which the Contractor intends to make from monies due to the Sub-Contractor [as provided for in clause 11(b) above] the Contractor shall give to the Sub-Contractor written notification of all such deductions not already notified in accordance with clause 11(b) above. Any such notification shall be given a reasonable time before the penultimate payment to the Sub-Contractor is due to be made.

(3)   In the event that, at the time of the Penultimate Payment, the total sum due from the Sub-Contractor to the Contractor (arising under sub-clauses 11(b)(1) and (2) hereof) exceeds the total of the sums due to the Sub-Contractor, there shall be a debt (for the difference) due from the Sub-Contractor to the Contractor. The Sub-Contractor shall pay such a debt within 7 working days of either the date when payment would otherwise have been due to the Sub-Contractor or of the notification by the Contractor of the debt, whichever is the later.

> **NOTE**
>
> The Employer's Representative is required, by the Main Contract, to issue the Penultimate Payment Certificate within five months of the date of substantial completion of the works. Within 20 working days of the issue by the Employer's Representative of the Penultimate Payment Certificate the Contractor shall pay the Sub-Contractor its Penultimate Payment.

11(j)   Final Payment

The Employer's Representative is required, by the Main Contract, to issue the Defects Certificate within 20 working days of the end of the Defects Period (which may have been extended in accordance with clause 8.6 ("Defects Period") of the Main Contract). The Employer's Representative is required, by the Main Contract, to issue the final payment certificate within three months of the issue of the Defects Certificate. Unless the Sub-Contractor's final account has been agreed and all payments due under it (including release of all retention) have been paid by the Contractor at an earlier date, within 20 working days of the issue by the Employer's Representative of the final payment certificate the Contractor shall pay the Sub-Contractor its final payment which shall be the sum due under this Sub-Contract and will include the final payment of retention, any amount due for additional works instructed after Substantial Completion, any amounts which were withheld from the Penultimate Payment and are now due and deduction of any sums due from the Sub-Contractor to the Contractor. The Contractor shall provide the Sub-Contractor with a statement with the final payment showing how the final payment sum has been computed.

11(k)   Taxes and Interest

The provisions in relation to Interest, Valued Added Tax and Withholding Tax in clauses 11.6 ("Time for Payment and Interest"), 11.7 ("Value Added Tax") and 11.8 ("Withholding Tax") of the Main Contract shall apply mutatis mutandis to the Sub-Contract. In so far however as an entitlement to interest arises in relation to payments certified under the Main Contract, the Sub-Contractor will only be entitled to a fair and reasonable proportion of such interest, if any, as is recovered by the Contractor.

12. TERMINATION

12(a) Termination on Sub-Contractor Default

The Contractor may, without limiting any other rights or remedies, terminate the Sub-Contract if any of the following occurs:-

   (i)   the Sub-Contractor in breach of contract fails to comply with its obligations under the Sub-Contract and, if the failure can be cured, the Sub-Contractor has failed to cure it within 10 days of being requested to do so by the Contractor;

   (ii) the Sub-Contractor abandons or suspends the execution of the Sub-Contract Works;

   (iii) the Sub-Contractor fails to proceed regularly and diligently with the execution of the Sub-Contract Works;

   (iv) the Sub-Contractor fails to provide or maintain the required insurances or performance bond;

   (v)   the Sub-Contractor or Sub-Contractor's Personnel has or displays a level of incompetence such that the warranty given by the Contractor in clause 2.5 ("Safety, Health and Welfare at Work Act 2005 and Safety, Health and Welfare at Work (Construction) Regulations 2006") of the Main Contract is rendered untrue or the Sub-Contractor's conduct is or has been such as to render the Contractor's warranty under clause 2.6 ("Ethics in Public Office") of the Main Contract untrue;

   (vi) the Sub-Contractor or Sub-Contractor's Personnel has committed or caused the Employer or the Contractor to commit a serious breach of Legal Requirements;

   (vii) the Sub-Contractor or Sub-Contractor's Personnel have committed a breach of the Safety, Health and Welfare at Work Act 2005 or any regulations or code of practice made under it;

   (viii) the Sub-Contractor or Sub-Contractor's Personnel has not complied with the requirements of clause 5(c) hereof either (a) within 10 days after notice from the Contractor requiring a failure to be put right or (b) persistently;

   (ix) the Sub-Contractor has sub-contracted all or any part of the Sub-Contract Works without the consent in writing of the Contractor;

   (x)   if any of the insolvency events referred to in clause 12.1 ("Termination on Contractor Default") of the Main Contract occur in relation to the Sub-Contractor. In this case, the Contractor will have the same rights and entitlements *mutatis mutandis* in relation to the Sub-Contractor as the Employer has in relation to the Contractor under clauses 12.1.2 and 12.1.3 of the Main Contract.

> **NOTE**
>
> Grounds for termination by the Contractor are as follows:
>
> * The Sub-Contractor in breach of contract fails to comply with its obligations under the sub-contract;
>
> * The Sub-Contractor abandons or suspends the execution of the works;
>
> * The Sub-Contractor fails to proceed regularly and diligently with the works;
>
> * The Sub-Contractor fails to provide or maintain the required insurances or performance bond;
>
> * Any of the Sub-Contractor's warranties given by the Sub-Contractor in sub-clause 2.5 ("Safety, Health and Welfare at Work Act 2005 and Safety, Health and Welfare at Work (Construction) Regulations 2006") or sub-clause 2.6 (Ethics in Public office) of the Main Contract are untrue;

- Committed or caused the Employer or the Contractor to commit a serious breach of Legal Requirements;

- Committed a breach of the Safety, Health and Welfare at Work Act 2005 or any regulations or code of practice made under it;

- The Sub-Contractor has not complied with the requirements of clause 5(c);

- The Sub-Contractor has sub-contracted all or any part of the sub-contract works without the consent in writing of the Contractor;

- Insolvency (8 events).

12(b) Consequences of Termination for Sub-Contractor Default

If the Sub-Contractor's obligation to complete the Sub-Contract Works is terminated under clause 12(a) hereof, the provisions of clause 12.2 ("Consequences of Default Termination") of the Main Contract will apply, *mutatis mutandis*, as between the Contractor and the Sub-Contractor as if all references to the Contractor therein were to the Sub-Contractor and all references to the Employer, or the Employer's Representative were to the Contractor. For the avoidance of doubt it is confirmed that references to Contractor's Things, Contractor's Documents, Works Items and Works shall be read as referring to Sub-Contractor's Things, Sub-Contractor's Documents, Sub-Contract Works Items and Sub-Contract Works respectively and that like terms applicable to the Main Contract will be changed, where the context admits or requires, to meet the purpose and intent of this Sub-Contract.

NOTE

The consequences of termination for Sub-Contractor default are:

- The Sub-Contractor leaves the site in an orderly manner;

- Payment of any monies due to the Sub-Contractor are postponed and the Contractor shall not be required to make any further payment to the Sub-Contractor except as provided in this clause;

- The Contractor, as soon as practicable, is to make an assessment of the amount due to the Sub-Contractor in respect of works completed in accordance with the contract and unpaid. This is the termination value;

- The Sub-Contractor cannot remove any work items or things from the site unless instructed to do so by the Contractor;

- The Contractor may engage other Sub-Contractors, use any work items and Sub-Contractor's things on the site and do any thing necessary for the completion of the works;

- If instructed by the Contractor, the Sub-Contractor shall assign to the Contractor, without further payment, the benefit of any sub-contract, contract for supply, or other contract in relation to the performance of the works;

- The Contractor may pay to any Sub-Contractor, or supplier to the Sub-Contractor, any amount due to it that the Contractor certifies as included in any previous interim payment. The Sub-Contractor shall re-pay to the Contractor such an amount on request;

- The Sub-Contractor provides to the Contractor all work requirements and Sub-Contractor's documents;

- When the works have been completed and the termination amount has been assessed, the Contractor shall certify the termination amount setting out:

  1. The Contractor's additional cost of completing the works compared with the cost that would have been incurred if the works had been completed by the Sub-Contractor;

  2. Loss and damage incurred by the Contractor as a result of the termination and its cause;

  3. Amounts due to the Contractor by the Sub-Contractor.

If the *termination amount* is less than the *termination value* the Sub-Contractor shall raise an invoice for the difference and the Contractor shall pay that amount within 15 days of receipt of the invoice. If the termination amount is more than the termination value the Sub-Contractor shall pay to the Contractor the difference within 10 working days of receiving the Contractor's demand for payment.

12(c)   Termination of the Contractor's Employment under clause 12.1 ("Termination on Contractor Default") of the Main Contract

(1)   If the Contractor's employment is terminated by the Employer under clause 12.1 ("Termination on Contractor Default") of the Main Contract, this Sub-Contract will automatically terminate.

(2)   If the termination of the Main Contract had been caused by default on the part of the Sub-Contractor, the Sub-Contractor shall be liable in damages to the Contractor for the loss suffered. Subject to the foregoing, if the validity of such termination is not disputed by the Contractor under the disputes resolution provisions of the Main Contract, or if it is disputed but the right of termination is upheld by a binding decision of a conciliator or arbitrator or court, the Contractor will indemnify the Sub-Contractor in relation to all loss and damage incurred by it by reason of the termination.

(3)   If the validity of the termination is successfully disputed by the Contractor with the effect that the Employer is held by a binding decision of a conciliator, arbitrator or court not to have been entitled to terminate, the Contractor shall take whatever steps are reasonable to recover any losses sustained by the Sub-Contractor on foot of the termination and will pay to the Sub-Contractor the proportion of any sum recovered from the Employer in relation to the termination as is referable to the Sub-Contractor's losses or, in the event of a settlement or outcome to the dispute does not clearly define the sum payable in relation to the Sub-Contractor's losses, such proportion of the sum recovered by the Contractor as is just and reasonable in all the circumstances. In assessing what is just and reasonable, regard will be had to any reduction in the amount which might have been otherwise recoverable by the Contractor against the Employer as a result of clause 12.9 ("Reference to Conciliation") of the Main Contract. The Contractor shall provide such information as is reasonably required by the Sub-Contractor to demonstrate the Contractor's compliance with this clause.

12(d)   Termination by the Sub-Contractor

The Sub-Contractor shall be entitled to terminate the Sub-Contractor's obligation to complete the Sub-Contract Works by notice to the Contractor in writing if any of the following occur:-

(i)   the Sub-Contractor has suspended the execution of the Sub-Contract Works for 15 working days in accordance with clause 11(d) hereof and the Contractor has still not paid.

(ii)   work has been suspended by direction of the Employer's Representative under sub-clause 9.2 ("Suspension") of the Main Contract and a right to terminate has arisen in favour of the Contractor under that sub-clause

(iii)   the execution of the Sub-Contract Works or a substantial part of the Sub-Contract Works has been suspended for a period of at least three months as a consequence of loss or damage that is at the Employer's risk under clause 3.1 ("Employer's Risks of Loss and Damage to the Works") of the Main Contract

(iv)   an event or circumstances outside the control of the parties makes it physically impossible or contrary to Law for the Sub-Contractor to fulfil its obligations under the Sub-Contract for a period of at least six months.

(v)   If the Contractor becomes insolvent as defined in clause 12.1.1 (11) of the Main Contract and the Employer has not terminated the Main Contract under clause 12.1 ("Termination on Contractor Default") thereof.

NOTE

The Sub-Contractor may terminate by notice to the Contractor if:

- The Sub-Contractor has suspended the Sub-Contract works for 15 working days in accordance with clause 11(d) and the Contractor has still not paid;

- Work has been suspended by direction of the Employer's Representative under sub-clause 9.2 ("Suspension") of the Main Contract and a right to terminate has arisen in favour of the Contractor under that sub-clause.

- Work or a substantial part of it has been suspended for a period of at least three months as a consequence of loss or damage that is at the Employer's risk under clause 3.1 ("Employer's Risks of Loss and Damage to the Works") of the Main Contract;

- An event outside the control of the parties makes it physically impossible or contrary to law for the Sub-Contractor to fulfil its obligations for a period of at least six months;

- If the Contractor becomes insolvent.

12(e) Consequences of Termination by Sub-Contractor or at Employer's Election

(1) If the Employer terminates the Main Contract under clause 12.5 ("Termination at Employer's Election") of the Main Contract that termination will automatically terminate the employment of the Sub-Contractor. In that event, or in the event of the Sub-Contractor terminating the Sub-Contract under clause 12(d)(i), (ii), (iii) or (iv) hereof, the following shall apply:-

   (i) The Sub-Contractor shall leave the site in an orderly manner and remove any Sub-Contractor's Things

   (ii) The Sub-Contractor shall give the Contractor all Works Requirements and all Sub-Contractor's Documents

   (iii) The Sub-Contractor shall as soon as practicable provide to the Contractor a statement of the total of the following (the **termination sum**):-

   - the unpaid value of the Sub-Contract Works completed to the date of termination and valued in accordance with clause 11(a) hereof

   - the Sub-Contractor's reasonable costs of removal from the Site as a consequence of the termination

   - all other amounts due to the Sub-Contractor under the Sub-Contract (but not damages)

The Contractor will take all reasonable measures to recover for the Sub-Contractor from the Employer payment in respect of the Sub-Contract Works and shall pay to the Sub-Contractor a fair and reasonable proportion of any sum recovered by the Contractor from the Employer in relation to the termination. If the termination sum indicates that money is due by the Sub-Contractor to the Contractor, the same will be paid forthwith by the Sub-Contractor to the Contractor. The Contractor shall provide such information as is reasonably required by the Sub-Contractor to demonstrate the Contractor's compliance with this sub-clause.

(2) Termination by the Sub-Contractor under clause 12(d)(i) or (v) constitutes a termination by reason of the Contractor's default or breach of contract and the Sub-Contractor will be entitled to be compensated in accordance with 10(c)(1) hereof.

NOTE

For the consequences of termination by Sub-Contractor or at the Employer's election. The following shall apply:

- The Sub-Contractor shall leave the site in an orderly manner and remove any Sub-Contractor's things;

- The Sub-Contractor shall give the Contractor all works requirements and all Sub-Contractor's documents.

The Sub-Contractor shall as soon as practicable provide to the Contractor a statement of the total of the following (*the termination sum*):

- The unpaid value of the sub-contract works completed to the date of termination;

- The Sub-Contractor's reasonable costs of removal from the site as a consequence of the termination;

- All other amounts due to the Sub-Contractor under the sub-contract (but not damages);

The Contractor will take all reasonable measures to recover for the Sub-Contractor from the Employer payment in respect of the sub-contract works and shall pay to the Sub-Contractor a fair and reasonable proportion of any sum recovered by the Contractor from the Employer in relation to the termination.

Termination by the Sub-Contractor under clause 12(d)(i) or (v) constitutes a termination by reason of the Contractor's default or breach of contract and the Sub-Contractor will be entitled to be compensated in accordance with 10(c)(1).

12(f) Survival

Termination of the Sub-Contractor's obligation to complete the Sub-Contract Works shall not affect the Sub-Contractor's obligations under the Sub-Contract, (other than the obligation to complete the Sub-Contract Works, after termination) and in particular the obligations of the Contractor which survive the termination of the Main Contract under clause 12.7 ("Survival") thereof shall continue to apply to the Sub-Contractor, in so far as they relate to the Sub-Contract, after termination.

13.   DISPUTES

13(a)   Notice to Refer

(1)   If a dispute arises between the parties in connection with or arising out of the Sub-Contract, either party may, by notice to the other, refer the dispute for arbitration by serving on the other a Notice to Refer. The Notice to Refer shall state the issues in dispute. The service of the Notice to Refer will be deemed to be the commencement of arbitration proceedings. Either party may within a period of 21 days of the Notice to Refer give notice to the other of further disputes and, if such notice is given, those further disputes will be deemed to be included in the reference to arbitration.

(2)   If the Notice to Refer is served by the Sub-Contractor, and the Contractor is of the view that the issues in dispute relate in whole or in part to a dispute between the Contractor and the Employer, provided the Contractor so indicates by notice to the Sub-Contractor in writing within 21 days of service of the Notice to Refer, the dispute, as between the Contractor and the Sub-Contractor in respect of those issues will be dealt with under sub-clause 13(d) hereof.

(3)   Except to the extent that the disputes which are the subject matter of the Notice to Refer have been the subject of notice served by the Contractor under the preceding sub-clause 13(a)(2) hereof, no step will be taken in the arbitration after the Notice to Refer has been served until the disputes have first been referred to mediation and, if mediation does not resolve the dispute, then to conciliation.

> **NOTE**
>
> If a dispute arises between the parties in connection with or arising out of the sub-contract, either party may, by notice to the other, refer the dispute for arbitration by serving on the other a Notice to Refer. The Notice to Refer shall state the issues in dispute. The service of the Notice to Refer will be deemed to be the commencement of arbitration proceedings.

13(b)   Mediation

(1)   Either party may activate the mediation process by giving written notice to the other party seeking the appointment of a mediator at any time after the expiry of 21 days from service of the Notice to Refer.

(2)   If the parties are unable to agree upon a person to act as mediator within a period of 15 working days of the notice seeking the appointment of a mediator, either party may apply to the President for the time being of the Construction Industry Federation who shall appoint a mediator. If there is a fee for making the appointment, the parties shall share it equally. Once a mediator has been appointed to a dispute between the parties, unless the parties agree otherwise, the same mediator shall deal with all other disputes between the parties, provided he/she is agreeable to do so. The mediation shall be conducted in accordance with the Mediation Procedure included in the Appendix Part 4 to this sub-contract.

> **NOTE**
>
> Sub-clause 13(b) introduces mediation as the first stage of the dispute resolution procedure. Either party may activate mediation process after the expiry of 21 days from the service of the Notice to Refer. Failing agreement by the parties in the appointment of a mediator, the Construction Industry Federation is the appointing body. The appointment fee is shared equally. The mediation procedure is contained in Appendix Part 4 was discussed previously.

13(c) Conciliation

(1) If the mediation is concluded without the dispute(s) having been resolved, either party may activate the conciliation process by giving written notice to the other party seeking the appointment of a conciliator. If the parties fail to agree a conciliator within 15 working days of the notice seeking the appointment of a conciliator, either party may apply to the President for the time being of the Construction Industry Federation who shall appoint a conciliator. If there is a fee for making the appointment, the parties shall share it equally.

(2) The provisions of sub-clauses 13.1.3 to 13.1.12 of clause 13.1 ("Conciliation"), of the Main Contract shall apply to the conciliation between the Contractor and Sub-Contractor (changing the word Employer to Contractor, the word Contractor to Sub-Contractor and the word Contract to Sub-Contract) with the exception of the final sentence of clause 13.1.9 (referral to arbitration following notice of dissatisfaction) and the second sentence of clause 13.1.10 (referral to arbitration of failure by one party to comply with a Conciliator's recommendation in respect of which neither party gave notice of dissatisfaction). Also, sub-clause 13.1.11 of the Main Contract will only apply if either or both of the parties has given notice of dissatisfaction.

(3) If notice of dissatisfaction has been given as provided for in clause 13.1.9 (of the Main Contract), either party may proceed to have the issues the subject matter of the Notice to Refer resolved through arbitration.

(4) If a party fails to comply with a conciliator's recommendation which is binding, the other party may take such court proceedings as are appropriate to force compliance with the conciliator's recommendation without availing further of the conciliation or arbitration process.

> **NOTE**
>
> Any dispute can be referred to conciliation during the course of the contract. If the dispute is not resolved within 42 days after the appointment of the conciliator, the conciliator shall make his recommendation. The parties have 45 days to accept the recommendation. If the recommendation is rejected by either party the matter can be referred to arbitration.
>
> If the recommendation stated that a sum of money should be paid by one party to the other then that shall be binding in the interim. The receiving party will have to provide a bond for the amount it receives.
>
> Any dispute referred to conciliation shall be finally settled by arbitration subject to the arbitration rules stated in the works requirements.

13(d) Joint Disputes

Any disputes the subject matter of the Contractor's notice under sub-clause 13(a)(2), hereof will be dealt with jointly with the dispute under the Main Contract on the following basis:-

(i)   the Contractor shall pursue the issue or issues in dispute under the Main Contract diligently

(ii)   the Sub-Contractor shall furnish the Contractor with all necessary information and documents in its possession in a timely manner and shall participate in and provide all necessary assistance for the preparation of submissions and pleadings and will indemnify the Contractor in respect of any loss or expense incurred as a result of the Sub-Contractor's failure to do so

(iii) the Contractor shall consult with the Sub-Contractor in regard to all pleadings and procedural matters in pursuing the dispute

(iv)   the Contractor shall ensure that the views of the Sub-Contractor in relation to the disputes, in so far as they relate to the Sub-Contract, are transmitted to any conciliator or arbitrator appointed in relation to the dispute and will, as far as practicable, safeguard the interests of the Sub-Contractor

(v)   the Sub-Contractor shall indemnify the Contractor in relation to any costs incurred in any such conciliation or arbitration to the extent that this is fair and reasonable having regard to the respective financial interests of the parties in relation to the issues in dispute and all other relevant circumstances. The Sub-Contractor will make such payments on account as the conciliation or arbitration proceeds as are reasonably sought by the Contractor

(vi) the Contractor and the Sub-Contractor will be bound by the outcome of any such binding conciliation or arbitration between the Employer and Contractor in so far as it relates to disputes connected with the Sub-Contract

NOTE

If the Notice to Refer is served by the Sub-Contractor, and the Contractor is of the view that the issues in dispute relate in whole, or in part, to a dispute between the Contractor and the Employer, provided the Contractor so indicates by notice to the Sub-Contractor in writing within 21 days of service of the Notice to Refer, the dispute, as between the Contractor and the Sub-Contractor, in respect of those issues, will be dealt with under sub-clause 13(c).

13(e) Arbitration

(1)   Except in the case of a dispute to which sub-clause 13(d) hereof applies, the parties shall jointly appoint the arbitrator and, if the parties are unable to agree an arbitrator to be appointed under this clause, the arbitrator will be appointed by the President for the time being of the Construction Industry Federation. The appointment of a conciliator or arbitrator when Clause 13(d) applies will be made in accordance with the Main Contract.

(2)   Any arbitration [other than under clause 13(d) hereof] between the Contractor and the Sub-Contractor will be governed by the Arbitration Procedure 2000 published by Engineers Ireland and will be subject to the Arbitration Acts 1954–1998.

APPENDIX

PART 1
to be completed by the Contractor before tenders are invited

> **NOTE**
>
> Part 1 consists of sections A–K.

A MAIN CONTRACT

The Main Contract Conditions are ....
....
....
Agreement Recitals Item A

> **NOTE**
>
> This sets out what the conditions of the Main Contract are.

B SUB-CONTRACT DOCUMENTS

Additional Documents relating to the Sub-Contract Works
Article 5 of Agreement

1.   ....
2.   ....
3.   ....
4.   ....
5.   ....

> **NOTE**
>
> Any additional documents relating to the sub-contract works are listed. Reference is made to Article 5 of the agreement.

C INSURANCES

Public Liability and Employer's Liability Insurance
Clauses 3 (d) (2) and 3 (d) (3)

Minimum indemnity limits for public liability and Employers' liability insurance:

- public liability insurance: €............................. for any one event, but this limit may be on an annual aggregate basis for products liability, collapse, vibration, subsidence, removal and weakening of supports and sudden and accidental pollution. (If not stated, €6,500,000).

- Employer's liability insurance: €............................. for any one event. (If not stated, €13,000,000).

Maximum excess for Insurance:

- public liability: €.. in respect of property damage only (If not stated, €10,000). There shall be no excess for death, injury or illness.

- Employer's liability: no excess.

Permitted exclusions from the Insurances:

The Sub-Contractor's insurance policies may include only the exclusions permitted Under the Main Contract as detailed in the Schedule Part 1 D thereof.

Professional Indemnity Insurance
Clause 3 (e)

Professional indemnity insurance is/is not (*delete one*) required. (If neither deleted, professional indemnity insurance is not required). If required, the professional indemnity insurance is to be kept in place for .... years after Substantial Completion of the Works is certified by the Employer's Representative (If not stated, 6 years). If Professional Indemnity Insurance is required, the minimum indemnity limit for professional indemnity insurance shall be €........................ for each and every claim or series of claims arising from the same originating cause/annual aggregate limit (*delete one*). The maximum excess shall be €..................... (If none stated, €50,000).

NOTE

Details of the insurance requirements under the contract will be listed here: public/products liability; Employer's liability insurance; public liability insurance; private/commercial motors; and other ancillary covers. Professional indemnity may be required and is referred to under clause 3(e).

Reference is made to the Schedule, Part 1 D of the Main Contract.

D   THE SITE
Clause 7 (c)

Method of Measurement:
The Method of Measurement defining the general attendances is
....[1]
(if left blank, the Method of Measurement (if any) defined in the Schedule part 1 B of the Main Contract will apply or (if none so defined) the Method of Measurement most commonly used in Ireland for the type of work being constructed in this case.

Special Attendances to be provided by the Contractor:-

1.   ....
2.   ....
3.   ....
4.   ....
5.   ....

NOTE

The method of measurement is specified and the Sub-Contractor should list any special attendances to be provided by the main Contractor.

E   PERFORMANCE BOND
Clause 1(h)

A Performance Bond is / is not (*DELETE ONE*) required. If neither is deleted a Performance Bond is not required.

F   COLLATERAL WARRANTY
Clause 5(e)

A Collateral Warranty is / is not (*DELETE ONE*) required from the Sub-Contractor. If neither is deleted a Collateral Warranty is not required.

---

[1] This should be the same as the Method of Measurement (if any) specified in the Schedule Part 1 B of the Main Contract.

G   TIME AND COMPLETION

Starting Date
Clause 9(a)

Period following receipt of a written instruction from the Contractor within which the Sub-Contractor must commence work on site .... working days (if left blank the period is 10 working days).

> **NOTE**
>
> This section provides the starting date in accordance with clause 9(a). The Sub-Contractor shall commence work within the specified period of receipt of a written instruction from the Contractor. If there is no time specified in the sub-contract then 10 working days applies.

H   PRICE VARIATION[2]
Clause 10(d)

Price Variation will apply in relation to the Sub-Contract Sum as follows:-

....

....

....

....

....

(if left blank, the Sub-Contract Sum is fixed).

> **NOTE**
>
> If left blank the sub-contract is fixed price.

I   CONTRACTOR'S RISK EVENTS

The Contractor will compensate the Sub-Contractor in respect of the following events (which are not Compensation Events under the Main Contract):-

....

....

....

> **NOTE**
>
> The Contractor will compensate the Sub-Contractor in respect of items that are not compensation events under the Main Contract are listed here.

J   SUB-CONTRACTOR'S RISK EVENTS

The Contractor will not compensate the Sub-Contractor in respect of the following events (irrespective of whether they are Compensation Events under the Main Contract):-

....

....

....

---

[2] The Contractor should take due account of the price fluctuation provisions which apply under the Main Contract in completing this item in the Appendix. The Contractor should note that, irrespective of the entry here, Clause 10(d) of the Sub-Contract provides that the Sub-Contract Sum is adjustable for Change in Law (on the assumption that the Main Contract has not been amended so than neither PV1 nor PV2 is included in it).

> **NOTE**
>
> The Contractor will not compensate the Sub-Contractor in respect of events, irrespective of whether they are compensation events under the Main Contract are listed here.

K   RETENTION
Clause 11(f)

[if this Section is left blank, retention will be deducted and released in accordance with Clauses 11(f)(i) and 11(f)(ii)]

Retention shall be deducted from interim payments to the Sub-Contractor at the rate of ....% subject to a limit of €...

The first moiety of the retention shall be released to the Sub-Contractor[3]

....

....

....

....

The second moiety of the retention shall be released to the Sub-Contractor

....

....

....

....

<u>Optional release of second moiety of retention in exchange for retention bond:</u>

The final (second) moiety of the retention **shall / shall not***
be released to the Sub-Contractor at the time of release of the first moiety provided the Sub-Contractor provides a retention bond from an insurance company or bank approved by the Contractor and in a form which is either approved by the Contractor or is in the form included in the Appendix Part 3 hereto. In neither case shall the Contractor's approval be unreasonably withheld.

*delete as applicable – if neither deleted "shall not" will apply

> **NOTE**
>
> The percentage amount of retention, the limit on retention and the release of retention monies are detailed here.

<u>VERY IMPORTANT NOTE</u>

The Contractor should also provide to tendering Sub-Contractors a copy of all relevant documentation from the Main Contract including (as appropriate) the completed Schedule or parts thereof.

> **NOTE**
>
> The Contractor shall also provide to the tendering Sub-Contractor a copy of all relevant documentation from the Main Contract including as appropriate the completed Schedule or parts thereof.

---

[3] It is suggested that a suitable entry would be "after the Sub-Contract Works are substantially complete at the next date for payment".

PART 2
to be completed by Sub-Contractor and submitted with tender

ADJUSTMENTS TO THE SUB-CONTRACT SUM INCLUDING DELAY COSTS
Clause 10 (b) (5)

The Sub-Contractor's tendered hourly rates for labour and related costs [including PRSI, benefits, tool money, travelling time and country money]:

- Craftspersons   €............... per hour

- General Operatives   €............... per hour

- Apprentices   €............... per hour

(If left blank, or stated as a negative value, read as zero)

The Sub-Contractor's tendered percentage addition for costs of materials..............%

The Sub-Contractor's tendered percentage addition/deduction for costs of plant................. %

All of the above shall include on-costs, overheads and profit, and exclude VAT. (If either of the above is left blank, read as zero.)

The Sub-Contractor's tendered rate of delay costs is €.............. excluding VAT per Site Working Day. (If left blank, or stated as a negative value, read as zero.)

If part 1K of the Schedule to the Main Contract states that separate rates are to be tendered for separate periods or parts of the Works, the Sub-Contractor's tendered rates are as follows:

Period or part of the Works (part 1K of Main Contract)	Tendered Rate
•	€.................. per site working day
•	€.................. per site working day
•	€.................. per site working day

Clause 10(b)(5)(iii)

Hourly rates for items of plant which are not listed in the document specified in Section K of the Schedule Part 1 of the Main Contract

Item of plant	Hourly Rate (€)

Percentage additions to the cost of materials and plant will also have to be quoted.

Sub-clause 10 (c) of the sub-contract requires the Sub-Contractor to state the amount per day he will be recompensed for delays.
An example of a delay cost per day would be:
Sub-Contractor's average daily delay cost

	€	
Staff	3,000	
Plant	1,000	
General Labour	1,000	
Overheads	1,000	
Insurances	500	
Any other	1,000	
Sub Total		€ 7,500
Designer/consultant		€ 1,000
To Tender		€ 8,500

The amount quoted by the Sub-Contractor in Appendix Part 2 is the amount that the contract sum is adjusted by regardless of whether or not the Sub-Contractor's costs are covered. This is the Sub-Contractor's risk.

In the event that the Sub-Contractor leaves the delay cost blank then the amount is taken as zero.

PART 3

Retention Bond

We, ... understand that under the terms of your Contract ("**the Contract**") with .... (hereinafter called "**the Applicant**") of .... for the .... entered into on .... you are retaining the sum of €............................... (say ....) the Contract value by way of the second moiety of retention monies ("**the Retention Monies**") and that you are prepared to release the said Retention Monies against a guarantee.

In consideration of your releasing the sum of €... to the Applicant, we .... hereby guarantee the repayment to you on demand of up to €....................(say ....…........................…..) in the event of the Applicant failing to fulfil the said Contract, provided that your claim hereunder is received in writing at this office accompanied by your signed statement that:-

1. the Applicant has failed to fulfil his obligations under the terms of the Contract,

   and

2. the Applicant has been advising in writing at least 30 (thirty) days before the date of your claim of the obligations of the Contract which have not been fulfilled and your intention to claim payment under this guarantee.

This guarantee shall remain valid until close of business at this office on the date on which, in the absence of this guarantee, the second moiety of retention would have become payable to the Applicant ("**Expiry**") subject to any matter of claim in dispute with the Applicant notified to this office before Expiry. Any claim hereunder must be received in writing at this office before Expiry accompanied by your signed statement as aforesaid, and such claim and statement shall be accepted as conclusive evidence that the amount claimed is due to you under this guarantee.

Claims and statements as aforesaid must bear the dated confirmation of your Bankers that the signatories thereon are authorised so to sign.

This guarantee shall become operative upon receipt of the Retention Monies by the Applicant.

Upon Expiry, the guarantee shall become null and void, whether returned to us for cancellation or not and any claim or statement received after Expiry shall be ineffective.

This guarantee is personal to yourselves and is not transferable or assignable, except by agreement which agreement shall not be unreasonably withheld.

This guarantee shall be governed by and construed in accordance with the Laws of Ireland and shall be subject to the exclusive jurisdiction of the Irish Courts.

Arbitration Clause

If either party to this bond shall be aggrieved regarding matters covered by this guarantee the party so aggrieved shall forthwith by notice in writing to the other refer such dispute or difference to arbitration of a person to be agreed upon between the parties or (if the parties fail to appoint an arbitrator within one calendar month of service of the notice as aforesaid) a person to be appointed on application of either party by the President for the time being of the Construction Industry Federation and such arbitrator shall forthwith and with all due expedition enter upon the reference and make an award thereon which award shall be final and conclusive. If the arbitrator declines the appointment or after appointment is removed by order of a competent Court or is incapable of acting or dies and the parties do not within one calendar month of the vacancy arising fill the vacancy then the President for the time being of Construction Industry Federation may on application of either party appoint an arbitrator to fill the vacancy. In any case where the President for the time being of Construction Industry Federation is not able to exercise the aforesaid functions conferred upon him the said function may be exercised on his behalf by the Vice President for the time being of the said Construction Industry Federation.

Executed as a Deed this .... day of ....20......

The Common Seal of ....

Was hereunto affixed in the presence of

....

....

....

NOTE
This is the retention bond and facilitates early release of retention monies.

PART 4

Mediation Procedure

1. This procedure shall apply to any mediation under Clause 13(b) of the Conditions of Sub-Contract for use with the Forms of Main Contract for Public Works issued by the Department of Finance 2007.

2. Within ten working days of appointment, the mediator shall contact both parties to arrange for a mediation meeting for the purpose of resolving the dispute, such meeting to take place within a further ten working days. Mediation is a flexible process and may be conducted in the manner the Mediator considers most appropriate. The Mediator may meet the parties either together or separately at the Mediator's discretion.

3. At least five working days prior to the mediation meeting each of the parties will supply to the mediator a concise summary of its position in relation to the matters in dispute, appending copies of the relevant documents. These summaries will not be exchanged between the parties or disclosed by the mediator except with the consent of the parties.

4. The mediator may consider and discuss such solutions to the dispute as he/she thinks appropriate or as may be suggested by either party. All information given to the mediator is confidential and shall remain so unless authorised by the party who supplied the information.

5. The mediation is confidential and all involved shall respect this confidentiality. Mediations are settlement negotiations and are without prejudice to the rights of the disputants. The summaries submitted to the Mediator in accordance with Clause 3, all written submissions, statements made, offers or proposals for settlement (made orally or in writing) in connection with the mediation shall be privileged and it shall not be permissible for the other party (not the author or originator of the document, statement, offer or proposal) to use or refer to such items in any subsequent conciliation, arbitration or legal proceedings (except as may be expressly agreed between the parties). Similarly, in any subsequent conciliation, arbitration or legal proceedings, it shall not be permissible for either party to use of refer to any proposals put forward by the Mediator during the Meditation.

6. The disputants agree not to summon or otherwise require the mediator to appear or testify or produce records, notes or any other information or material in any legal proceedings, in court or arbitration, and no recording or stenographic records will be made of the mediation.

7. Each party to the mediation shall pay its own costs. The parties shall be jointly and severally liable for the mediator's fees and costs and shall discharge these in equal shares.

8. Any agreement reached by the parties through the mediation shall be set down in writing and duly executed by their authorised representatives and shall not otherwise be legally binding.

9. In the event of the parties failing to reach settlement, the mediation will terminate when the mediator, at his absolute discretion, so decides or when the parties agree. Upon such termination either party will be entitled immediately to commence conciliation.

NOTE

This is the mediation procedure introduced as the first stage for the resolution of disputes. Mediation is a quick, efficient and economical process. The procedure provides that within 10 working days of appointment, the mediator contacts the parties and sets a date for a meeting which is to take place within a further 10 working days. Summary statements are to be submitted to the mediator at least five working days before the meeting takes place. The statements will not be exchanged or disclosed without the consent of the parties.

PART II

AGREEMENT
AND
CONDITIONS OF SUB-CONTRACT (NN)

FOR USE IN CONJUNCTION WITH THE FORMS OF MAIN CONTRACT FOR PUBLIC WORKS ISSUED BY THE DEPARTMENT OF FINANCE 2007 WHERE THE SUB-CONTRACTOR IS A SPECIALIST WHO HAS BEEN NAMED BY THE EMPLOYER OR WHOSE CONTRACT WITH THE EMPLOYER HAS BEEN NOVATED ("NN SUB-CONTRACTOR")

This form of sub-contract is issued by the
Construction Industry Federation,
Construction House, Canal Road, Dublin

CONTENTS OF PART II

AGREEMENT

THIS AGREEMENT is made on

BETWEEN:-...

of...

....

(the Contractor)

and..

of...

....

(the NN Sub-Contractor)

WHEREAS:-

A. The Contractor has entered or will enter into a Contract (which is defined in the Appendix Part 1) with the Employer for the Works described in the Main Contract.

B. The NN Sub-Contractor has been named by the Employer in the Main Contract or the Employer has novated its contract with the NN Sub-Contractor and as a result the Contractor is obliged to engage the NN Sub-Contractor to complete the Sub-Contract Works.

C. The Contractor and the NN Sub-Contractor agree to enter into this Sub-Contract under the terms and conditions herein agreed.

THE CONTRACTOR AND THE NN SUB-CONTRACTOR AGREE AS FOLLOWS:-

Article 1: The NN Sub-Contractor shall execute and complete the Sub-Contract Works and otherwise comply with its obligations in accordance with the Sub-Contract Conditions.

Article 2: The Contractor shall pay the NN Sub-Contractor the Sub-Contract Sum subject to and in accordance with the Sub-Contract and shall comply with its other obligations in the Sub-Contract.

Article 3: The Initial Sub-Contract Sum including VAT is €   (
). The Initial Sub-Contract Sum is a lump sum and shall only be adjusted when the Sub-Contract says so.

Article 4: The NN Sub-Contractor has satisfied itself before entering into the Sub-Contract of all the circumstances that may affect the cost of executing and completing the Sub-Contract Works and of the correctness and sufficiency of the Initial Sub-Contract Sum to cover the cost of performing the Sub-Contract. The NN Sub-Contractor has included in the Initial Sub-Contract Sum allowances for all risks, customs, policies, practices, and other circumstances that may affect its performance of the Sub-Contract, whether they could or could not have been foreseen, except for events for which the Sub-Contract provides for adjustment of the Initial Sub-Contract Sum.

Article 5: The Sub-Contract consists of the following documents:-
*   This Agreement;
*   The attached Conditions of Sub-Contract and completed Appendix Parts 1 and 2;
*   The Main Contract Documents in so far as these relate to the Sub-Contract Works;
*   The additional documents identified in the Appendix Part 1 hereto as relating specifically to the Sub-Contract Works;
*   Any Novated Design Documents;

Present when the Common Seal of THE CONTRACTOR
was affixed hereto:

....

Present when the Common Seal of the NN SUB-CONTRACTOR
was affixed hereto:

....

OR

Signed by an Authorised Representative of the CONTRACTOR

....

in the presence of .... (Witness)

Address of Witness ....

....

Signed by an Authorised Representative of the NN SUB-CONTRACTOR

....

in the presence of .... (Witness)

Address of Witness ....

....

NOTE

The first part of the sub-contract sets out the Articles of Agreement. This is the basic Contract and describes what the Sub-Contractor agrees to do and the price the Contractor agrees to pay to the Sub-Contractor. The Articles of Agreement set out the fundamental relationship between the Contractor and the Sub-Contractor.

There are five Articles expressing the sub-contract. Between them they establish that in exchange for the "sub-contract sum" the Sub-Contractor will carry out the sub-contract works in accordance with the sub-contract documents. Article 4 sets out that, in calculating the "initial sub-contract sum" the Sub-Contractor has taken into account "allowances for all risks, customs, policies, practices, and other circumstances that may affect its performance of the Sub-Contract, whether they could or could not have been foreseen, except for events for which the Sub-Contract provides for adjustment of the Initial Sub-Contract Sum" unless the sub-contract specifies otherwise. The initial sub-contract sum is inserted as VAT inclusive and is referred to as a lump sum to be adjusted only when the sub-contract says so.

CONDITIONS

1. THE SUB-CONTRACT

1(a) Definitions

In this Sub-Contract unless the context otherwise requires:-

Compensation Event means an event which is so designated in the table in Section K of the Schedule Part 1 of the Main Contract.

Initial Sub-Contract Sum means the sum tendered by the NN Sub-Contractor and accepted by the Contractor, including any adjustments agreed before acceptance.

NN Sub-Contractor means a Specialist who has been named by the Employer or whose contract with the Employer has been novated to the Contractor.

NN Sub-Contractor's Personnel means the employees and other persons, including sub-contractors to the NN Sub-Contractor, working on or adjacent to the Site for the NN Sub-Contractor or subcontractors to the NN Sub-Contractor and other persons assisting the NN Sub-Contractor to perform the Sub-Contract.

NN Sub-Contractor's Things means equipment, facilities and other things the NN Sub-Contractor [or NN Sub-Contractor's Personnel] uses on or adjacent to the Site to execute the Sub-Contract Works, except Sub-Contract Works Items.

Novated Design Documents means specifications, drawings and other documents identified in the Appendix Part 1B or in the Schedule to the Main Contract, Part 1B that have been made by the NN Sub-Contractor.

Sub-Contract Documents means the documents so identified in Article 5 of the Sub-Contract Agreement.

Sub-Contract Sum means the value of the Sub-Contract works calculated in accordance with these Conditions of Sub-Contract.

Sub-Contract Works means that portion of the Works which are to be constructed by the NN Sub-Contractor including, where applicable, any design to be carried out by the NN Sub-Contractor.

Sub-Contract Works Item means a part of the Sub-Contract Works, anything that the NN Sub-Contractor intends will become part of the Sub-Contract Works, or temporary works for the Sub-Contract Works.

Unfixed Sub-Contract Works Items means items of work which have not yet been incorporated in the Works.

Works means the works which are to be constructed under and in accordance with the Main Contract.

> **NOTE**
>
> Sub-contracting – key changes from the old contracts:
>
> - There are no PC Sums or nominated Sub-Contractors, only specialists who will be regarded as "domestic contractors";
>
> - The Contractor is responsible for the design by Specialists;
>
> - There is a provision for professional indemnity insurance;
>
> - There is a provision for collateral warranties;
>
> - Health and safety regulations are reflected in the contract conditions.

1(b)   Interpretation

(1)   The parties intend the Sub-Contract to be given purposeful meaning for efficiency and public benefit generally and as particularly identified in the Sub-Contract.

(2)   Words which are defined in clause 1.1 ("Definitions") of the Main Contract will have the same meaning when used in this Sub-Contract as in the Main Contract. The fact that a word is being used in its defined meaning will be indicated by the use of upper case printing in relation to the initial letters, irrespective of whether the words are defined in the Main Contract or the Sub-Contract.

(3)   The words and phrases to which interpretations are ascribed by clause 1.2.2 of the Main Contract have, unless the context indicates otherwise, the same interpretations in this Sub-Contract.

(4)   If the Sub-Contract includes a requirement for the NN Sub-Contractor to carry out design, the words "execute" and "execution" in respect of the Sub-Contract Works shall be deemed to include design irrespective of whether design is expressly stated or not.

(5)   Reference to any Act of the Oireachtas shall include any Act replacing that Act or amending it, and any Order, Regulation, Instrument, Directions, Scheme or Permission made under it or deriving validity from it.

(6)   The headings and index (including its references to the Main Contract) appearing in this Sub-Contract are for reference purposes only and shall not affect the construction or interpretation of this Sub-Contract.

1(c)   Assignment

The NN Sub-Contractor may not assign the benefit of the Sub-Contract, or any part of it, without the Contractor's consent.

1(d)   Period of Liability

If the Main Contract is executed under seal, the period of liability of the NN Sub-Contractor shall be twelve years.

1(e)   Execution of the Sub-Contract Works

The NN Sub-Contractor shall design (to the extent that this is the NN Sub-Contractor's responsibility), execute and complete the Sub-Contract Works to the reasonable satisfaction of the Contractor and in conformity with the reasonable directions and requirements of the Contractor.

1(f)   NN Sub-Contractor's Obligations

(1)   The NN Sub-Contractor will observe, perform and comply with all of the provisions of the Main Contract in so far as they relate and apply to the Sub-Contract Works (or any portion of the same) and are not repugnant to or inconsistent with the express provisions of this Sub-Contract as if all the same were severally set out herein.

(2)   The NN Sub-Contractor shall avoid through any neglect, omission or act on its part occasioning the Contractor to be in breach of any of the terms and provisions of the Main Contract. The NN Sub-Contractor is entitled to a copy of the documents comprising the Main Contract (the **Contract Documents**) in so far as these relate to the Sub-Contract Works. The NN Sub-Contractor however is not entitled to particulars relating to the Contractor's prices and these may be deleted from any documents to which the NN Sub-Contractor is entitled.

(3) The NN Sub-Contractor will deliver to the Contractor any notice, information or other requirement relating to the Sub-Contract Works, which the Contractor is entitled to or is required to furnish to the Employer's Representative, in sufficient time and detail as to enable the Contractor to meet the time requirements and other obligations of the Main Contract.

1(g) Damages for breach of the Sub-Contract

In the event that either party is in breach of the Sub-Contract the other party will be entitled to damages suffered as a consequence, provided due notification is given to the other party in accordance with the terms of the Sub-Contract.

1(h) Rights and Benefits under the Main Contract

So far as is lawfully permissible, the Contractor will, at the request and cost of the NN Sub-Contractor, obtain for the NN Sub-Contractor any rights or benefits of the Main Contract, only in so far as the same are applicable to the Sub-Contract.

1(i) Performance Bond / Sureties

(1) Before commencement on site, the NN Sub-Contractor will procure a bond from an insurance company or a bank approved by the Contractor (such approval not to be unreasonably withheld) guaranteeing the due performance of the Sub-Contract by the NN Sub-Contractor. The amount of the performance bond will be 25% of the Initial Sub-Contract Sum up to certification by the Employer's Representative of Substantial Completion of the Works and 12.5% of the Initial Sub-Contract Sum for the subsequent 15 months. The form of the bond will be subject to the approval of the Contractor, such approval not to be unreasonably withheld or delayed.

(2) The NN Sub-Contractor has the option of obtaining from the Contractor a surety to the value of 25% of the Initial Sub-Contract Sum for the benefit of the NN Sub-Contractor from an insurance company or a bank (the guarantor) guaranteeing that the Contractor will pay the NN Sub-Contractor in accordance with the terms of the Sub-Contract. In the event that the NN Sub-Contractor exercises this option, the Contractor will be entitled to recover from the NN Sub-Contractor half the cost of obtaining this payment guarantee up to a maximum of 0.2% of the Initial Sub-Contract Sum. The guarantor will be subject to the approval of the NN Sub-Contractor, such approval not to be unreasonably withheld or delayed. This payment guarantee shall be in the form included in the Appendix Part 3 hereto or in a form approved by the NN Sub-Contractor, such approval not to be unreasonably withheld or delayed[7]. The guarantee will only be enforceable against the guarantor in relation to sums that are due and remain unpaid for a period of 30 working days after the issue by the Employer's Representative of a certificate under Clause 11.1.3 of the Main Contract or 50 working days after the due date for submission of the Contractor's Interim Statement under Clause 11.1.1 of the Main Contract (whichever is the sooner). Upon expiry of that period the NN Sub-Contractor must give notice in writing to the Employer of its intention to make a claim under the payment guarantee and must afford the Contractor a period of fifteen working days from receipt of this notice to make payment. The NN Sub-Contractor shall not give notice to or otherwise contact the guarantor in relation to its intention to make such a claim prior to the expiry of the said period of fifteen working days. If the allegedly due debt is disputed by the Contractor the issue must be resolved through the disputes resolution procedure under Clause 13 before any payment will be made by the guarantor.

---

[7] If a form of payment guarantee other that that provided in the Appendix Part 3 is used, it should be consistent with the wording of clause 1(i)(2) and allow for the procedures incorporated in that clause.

1(j)   Works Requirements

Where the Main Contract is a public works contract for works designed by the Contractor, the NN Sub-Contractor is deemed to have satisfied itself before entering the sub-contract of the adequacy of the Works Requirements in so far as they relate to the Sub-Contract Works. The Contractor will not be liable to the NN Sub-Contractor for any deficiency in the Works Requirements and the NN Sub-Contractor is fully responsible for the adequacy of the works Requirements in so far as they relate to the Sub-Contract Works. The NN Sub-Contractor however will not be liable to the Contractor for either of the following:-

(i)   Statements in the Works Requirements of intended purpose of the Works or parts of them;

(ii)   Criteria in the Works Requirements for testing or performance of the completed Works or part of them;

NOTE

This clause sets out the general parameters and contains similar provisions compared with the existing contract forms: definitions, interpretation, assignment, period of liability, execution of the sub-contract works, NN Sub-Contractor's obligations, rights ands benefits under the main Contract, bonds and works requirements.

The provision for the bond is 25 percentage of the initial sub-contract sum up to certification of the substantial completion of the works and then reduces to 12.5 percentage of the initial sub-contract sum for the subsequent 15 months.

There is the provision for NN Sub-Contractor to request a surety 1 (i) (2). Reference is made to the payment guarantee in Appendix 3 and was commented on above. The cost of the guarantee is not free to the NN Sub-Contractor. The Contractor will be entitled to recover from the NN Sub-Contractor half the cost of obtaining the guarantee up to a maximum of 0.20 percentage of the initial sub-contract sum. The guarantor will be subject to the approval of the NN Sub-Contractor, such approval not to be unreasonably withheld or delayed.

2.   THE LAW

2(a)   Law Governing the Contract

Irish Law governs the Sub-Contract and its interpretation.

2(b)   Compliance with Legal Requirements

(1)   The NN Sub-Contractor shall in performing the Sub-Contract comply with all Legal Requirements.

(2)   The NN Sub-Contractor shall give and comply with all notices and pay all taxes, fees and charges required under Legal Requirements in connection with performing the Sub-Contract unless the Works Requirements say otherwise. Where such taxes, fees and charges relate in part to the Sub-Contract Works and in part to other works the same will be apportioned proportionately between the Contractor and the NN Sub-Contractor on a fair and reasonable basis.

2(c)   Consents

The Employer has obtained, or shall obtain the Consents the Works Requirements specify that the Employer is to obtain. The Contractor is obliged under the Main Contract to obtain all other Consents. In so far as such other Consents relate to the Sub-Contract Works, the NN Sub-Contractor shall obtain those Consents. If the Contractor is obliged to obtain Consents under the Main Contract which are required partly but not exclusively in relation to the Sub-Contract Works or to enable the NN Sub-Contractor to meet its obligations under this Sub-Contract, the cost of obtaining such Consents will be borne as between the Contractor and the NN Sub-Contractor on the basis of what is fair and reasonable having regard to the extent to which the Consents relate to the Sub-Contract Works and other works respectively. Any delay, loss or expense incurred by the Contractor and the NN Sub-Contractor in obtaining or failing to obtain such Consents will be borne in similar proportions respectively.

2(d)   Safety, Health and Welfare Statutory Requirements

(1)   The NN Sub-Contractor will comply with the Construction Regulations and will provide to the Contractor all documents required for the Safety File (as defined in the Construction Regulations) relevant to the Sub-Contract Works in sufficient time as to enable the Contractor meet its obligations under the Main Contract.

(2)   The NN Sub-Contractor (without limiting its other obligations) shall ensure, so far as is practicable, that the Sub-Contract Works:-

    (i)   are designed (to the extent that they are designed by the NN Sub-Contractor or the NN Sub-Contractor's Personnel) to be safe and are capable of being constructed safely and without risk to health and

    (ii)   are constructed in a safe manner and

    (iii)   are constructed to be safe and without risk to health and

    (iv)   can be maintained safely and without risk to health during use and

    (v)   comply in all respects, as appropriate, with the relevant statutory provisions;

(3)   The NN Sub-Contractor represents and warrants to the Contractor that the NN Sub-Contractor is, and will be, while performing this Sub-Contract, a competent person for the purpose of ensuring, so far as is reasonably practicable, that the Sub-Contract Works are as stated in sub-clause 2(d)(1).

NOTE

This clause contains general requirements in relation to compliance with legal requirements, consents and health and safety. It is worth noting that under clause 12.1.1.8 of the main Contract any breach of safety, health and welfare statutory requirements is a termination event. This applies to all Contractor's personnel including specialists and Sub-Contractors.

3. LOSS, DAMAGE AND INJURY

3(a) NN Sub-Contractor's Indemnities

(1) The NN Sub-Contractor will indemnify and save harmless the Contractor against and from any loss or expense incurred by the Contractor due to any failure on the part of the NN Sub-Contractor to observe the terms of this Sub-Contract or the terms of the Main Contract insofar as they apply to this Sub-Contract, including, where applicable, any liquidated damages (or charges made under Clause 7.12 of the Main Contract if applicable) the Contractor is obliged to pay to the Employer as a result of such failure.

(2) The NN Sub-Contractor will indemnify and save harmless the Contractor and the Employer in relation to any damage to the Works or to any property of the Contractor or of the Employer arising from or in the course of the NN Sub-Contractor's performance or non-performance of the Sub-Contract. The NN Sub-Contractor's liability under this sub-clause will not apply to the extent that the loss or damage arises from circumstances to which the Employer's indemnity under clause 3.5 ("Employer's Indemnity") of the Main Contract applies or to the extent that the same was caused by the negligence or default of the Contractor. Nor will the NN Sub-Contractor be liable for such loss and damage to the extent that it is occasioned by a risk which is that of the Employer under the Main Contract.

(3) The NN Sub-Contractor will indemnify and save harmless the Contractor and the Employer in respect of any loss arising as a result of:-

   (i) Death, injury or illness of any person including Sub-Contractor's Personnel but otherwise excluding Contractor's Personnel; and

   (ii) Destruction of or damage to any physical property (other than the Works); and

   (iii) Obstruction, loss of amenities, nuisance, trespass, stoppage of traffic and infringement of light, easement or quasi easement;

arising from or in the course of the performance or non-performance of the Sub-Contract. The NN Sub-Contractor's indemnity in relation to the death, injury or illness of NN Sub-Contractor's Personnel will apply regardless of whether the death, illness, or injury was caused wholly or in part by the negligence of any third party including the Contractor, the Contractor's Personnel or the Employer or the Employer's Personnel. Subject to the foregoing the NN Sub-Contractor will not be liable to indemnify the Contractor or the Employer in respect of the risks identified in sub-clauses (i), (ii) and (iii) above to the extent that the loss is caused by the negligence of the Contractor or the Employer or as a result of the risks in relation to which the Employer has indemnified the Contractor under clause 3.5 ("Employer's Indemnity") of the Main Contract or the risks assumed by the Employer under clauses 3.1 ("Employer's Risks of Loss and Damage to the Works") and 3.8 ("Existing Facilities and Use or Occupation by the Employer") thereof.

3(b) Obligation to Repair

In case of any loss or damage to the Sub-Contract Works, including any Sub-Contract Works Items, due to any event which is at the risk of the NN Sub-Contractor, including any loss or damage due to defective design by the NN Sub-Contractor, the NN Sub-Contractor shall proceed with due diligence to rectify such loss or damage at its own expense.

3(c) Insurance of the Works and NN Sub-Contractor's Things

(1) The Contractor shall for the benefit of itself and its Sub-Contractors (including the NN Sub-Contractor), as co-insured, keep in force in accordance with the requirements of the Main Contract a policy of insurance covering the Works and Works Items.

(2)   The NN Sub-Contractor shall take out insurance on terms and with an insurer approved by the Contractor (such approval not to be unreasonably withheld) of the NN Sub-Contractor's Things against destruction, loss and damage to their full reinstatement value.

(3)   The NN Sub-Contractor shall be deemed to have knowledge of all terms and conditions in the Contractor's policy of insurance covering the Works and the NN Sub-Contractor shall be entitled to inspect the said policy upon reasonable notice. The NN Sub-Contractor shall observe and comply with the conditions contained in the Contractor's policy of insurance covering the Works in so far as compliance is within the control of the NN Sub-Contractor. The NN Sub-Contractor will indemnify the Contractor in relation to any act or omission on the NN Sub-Contractor's part which causes the Contractor's said policy to become invalid or ineffective in whole or in part.

3(d)   Public Liability and Employer's Liability Insurance

(1)   Before commencing the Sub-Contract Works, the NN Sub-Contractor shall take out with an insurer approved by the Contractor (such approval not to be unreasonably withheld) Public Liability and Employer's Liability policies of insurance as provided herein. The NN Sub-Contractor will maintain such insurance until the Defects Certificate is issued by the Employer's Representative.

(2)   The minimum indemnity limits of these policies shall be the sums stated in the Appendix Part 1 hereto or, if no sums are so stated, shall be those sums stated in the Schedule Part 1D of the Main Contract.

(3)   The excesses in the NN Sub-Contractor's policies of insurance shall not exceed the sums stated in the Appendix Part 1 hereto or, if no sums are so stated shall not exceed the sums stated in the Schedule Part 1D of the Main Contract.

(4)   The said policies shall cover the NN Sub-Contractor's liability under statute and at common law and its liability to indemnify the Contractor under clause 3(a)(3) of this Sub-Contract.

(5)   The NN Sub-Contractor's public liability policy shall be issued in the joint names of the NN Sub-Contractor, the Contractor and the Employer and will contain cross liability clauses such that the policy shall operate as if a separate policy had been issued to each. If under the Main Contract the Contractor's public liability insurance is required to include as joint insured another party named by the Employer that party will also be a joint insured in the NN Sub-Contractor public liability insurance policy.

(6)   The NN Sub-Contractor's Employer's liability policy shall include a provision by which in the event of any claim in respect of which the NN Sub-Contractor would be entitled to receive indemnity under the policy being made against the Contractor or the Employer the insurer will indemnify the Contractor and the Employer against such claims and any costs, charges and expenses in respect thereof.

(7)   The NN Sub-Contractor may only include in its policies under this clause the exclusions permitted by the Main Contract in relation to the insurances taken out by the Main Contractor in so far as the same apply, *mutatis mutandis*, to the NN Sub-Contractor and / or to the Sub-Contract Work.

3(e)   Professional Indemnity Insurance

If the Appendix Part 1 hereto states that professional indemnity insurance is required in relation to the design of the Sub-Contract Works by the NN Sub-Contractor, the NN Sub-Contractor shall arrange such cover for the sum indicated by that Appendix Part 1 to commence with the commencement of the design of the Sub-Contract Works and to remain effective for a period of six years from substantial completion of the Works, unless otherwise stated in the Appendix Part 1 hereto. This insurance shall include retroactive cover to when the NN Sub-Contractor's design of the Sub-Contract Works and Sub-Contract Works Items started.

3(f)   Evidence of Insurance Cover

The NN Sub-Contractor shall provide written confirmation to the reasonable satisfaction of the Contractor of the existence of the insurance policies as required under this Sub-Contract and that the premium for each policy has been paid. Furthermore the NN Sub-Contractor shall obtain written confirmation from its insurers that the said insurers will notify the Contractor in the event of any amendment or cancellation of the said insurance policies (including the amount of any excess deductible therein contained).

3(g)   Owner Controlled Insurance Programme

If the Works Requirements include provision for an owner controlled insurance programme, the parties hereto shall comply with those provisions and this clause 3 shall be amended, as reasonably required, to give effect to such programme.

> **NOTE**
>
> These are the insurance clauses and are referred to in Part 1 of the Appendix. Clause 3 (e) refers to "Professional Indemnity Insurance". This is required for any NN Sub-Contractor designed works.

4. MANAGEMENT

> **NOTE**
>
> This is a significant area under the new contracts, as specific requirements in relation to the management of the project are set out.

4(a) Co-operation

The Contractor and the NN Sub-Contractor shall provide reciprocal co-operation and support for the Sub-Contract purposes. The provisions of clause 4.1. ("Co-operation") of the Main Contract shall apply as between the Contractor and NN Sub-Contractor in that regard.

> **NOTE**
>
> The Contractor and the NN Sub-Contractor shall provide reciprocal co-operation and support for the sub-contract purposes.

4(b) Instructions

(1) The Contractor may issue instructions to the NN Sub-Contractor in relation to any matter connected with the Sub-Contract Works (whether or not mentioned elsewhere in the Sub-Contract) at any time up to the date of issue of the Defects Certificate. The NN Sub-Contractor shall comply with the instructions of the Contractor.

(2) Instructions of the Contractor may vary the Sub-Contract Works (including by adding to, omitting and changing the Sub-Contract Works and imposing, removing and changing restrictions on how they are to be executed).

(3) Instructions by the Contractor shall be given in writing except when there is imminent danger to safety or health or of damage to property, in which case the Contractor may give oral instructions and shall confirm them in writing as soon as is practicable.

> **NOTE**
>
> The Contractor may issue instructions on any matter connected with the works at any time up to the date the defects certificate is issued. The NN Sub-Contractor must comply with all instructions. There is no facility for the Contractor to confirm verbal instructions or to work on verbal instructions unless for matters of health and safety. Instructions may vary the sub-contract works. All instructions should be reviewed to establish if they are "change orders". In the event of a change order been issued then it is a delay and compensation event under item 1 of section K of part 1 of the schedule of the main Contract.

4(c) Works Proposals & Required Contractor Submissions

To enable the Contractor fully to meet its obligations under clauses 4.6 ("Works Proposals") and 4.7 ("Required Contractor Submissions") of the Main Contract, the NN Sub-Contractor shall provide any required documents, information, design data or other data and will take all steps necessary in relation to the Sub-Contract Works. The NN Sub-Contractor is fully responsible for the accuracy and adequacy of the Novated Design Documents (if any) and fully indemnifies the Contractor for any loss sustained by it by reason of any defect in the design of the Sub-Contract Works undertaken by the NN Sub-Contractor.

> **NOTE**
>
> The NN Sub-Contractor is required to provide any documents, information, design data or other date and take all steps necessary in relation to the sub-contract works. The NN Sub-Contractor is

fully responsible for the accuracy and adequacy of the "novated design documents" (if any) and fully indemnifies the Contractor for any loss sustained by it by reason of any defect in the design of the sub-contract works undertaken by the NN Sub-Contractor.

4(d) Programme & Progress Reports

(1) The NN Sub-Contractor shall carry out and complete the Sub-Contract Works to meet the requirements of the Main Contract programme in compliance with sub-clause 4(d)(5) hereof.

(2) The NN Sub-Contractor shall liaise and cooperate with the Contractor and other sub-contractors (including NN Sub-Contractors) of the Contractor and / or other contractors of the Employer engaged on or in connection with the Works and shall so programme and order the Sub-Contract Works so that the Contractor and / or its NN Sub-Contractors and / or other contractors of the Employer are not delayed or disrupted.

(3) The Contractor shall give reasonable notice of any information it requires from the NN Sub-Contractor in respect of programming and progress of the Sub-Contract Works to enable the Contractor to meet its obligations under the Main Contract, including those set out at clauses 4.9 ("Programme") and 4.10 ("Progress Reports") and the NN Sub-Contractor shall provide the required information in such detail and in such time as will enable the Contractor to avoid being in breach of its obligations under the Main Contract.

(4) If required by the Contractor, the NN Sub-Contractor shall provide information for the Contractor's programme including the details of the following:-

  (i) when the NN Sub-Contractor will require any instructions, Works Items or any other things to be given by the Employer or the Contractor

  (ii) a programme showing the order in which the NN Subcontractor proposes to execute the Sub-Contract Works and the duration of the various Sub-Contract activities

  (iii) Details of procurement, manufacture, delivery, construction, testing and commissioning of the Sub-Contract Works Items and the sequence and timing of inspections and tests.

  (iv) Where the Main Contract is a public works contract for civil engineering works, the methods by which the NN Sub-Contractor proposes to execute the Sub-Contract Works and any temporary works.

(5) (i) The Sub-Contractor's programme shall allow reasonable periods of time for the Employer, the Employer's Personnel or the Contractor to comply with their respective obligations under the Main Contract and under the Sub-Contract

  (ii) The Sub-Contractor's programme shall comply with the Contractor's programme at all times and shall be revised from time to time, as necessary, to do so. The Contractor shall not revise its programme unreasonably or to an unreasonable extent.

  (iii) If at any time the Sub-Contractor's then applicable programme does not comply with the actual progress of the Sub-Contract Works or with the Sub-Contractor's obligations or the Contractor's obligations, the Sub-Contractor, if so directed by the Contractor, shall submit a revised programme which complies with this Sub-Contract and reflects the actual progress position at that time.

(6) The NN Sub-Contractor shall provide to the Contractor monthly progress reports from the commencement of the Sub-Contract Works until the completion thereof. The first report shall relate to the period from the commencement date up to the end of the month in which it occurs and each subsequent report shall relate to each subsequent month. The NN Sub-Contractor shall provide each progress report within four working days after the end of the month to which it relates. Each progress report shall be in the format required by the Contractor to meet its obligations under the Main Contract.

(7)   Each progress report shall include in relation to the Sub-Contract Works such detail as is reasonably required by the Contractor to meet its obligations under clause 4.10 ("Progress Reports"), sub-clause 4.10.2 of the Main Contract and shall include, unless the NN Sub-Contractor is informed otherwise in writing, the following;-

(i)   a detailed description of progress of each stage of the Sub-Contract Works

(ii)   the names of off-site suppliers in relation to the Sub-Contract Works, and the progress and location of the design, manufacture, fabrication, delivery, installation, testing and commissioning of Sub-Contract Works Items

(iii) details of the NN Sub-Contractor's Personnel and NN Sub-Contractor's Things on the Site

(iv)   status of preparation and review of Sub-Contract Documents

(v)   copies of quality assurance documents and tests results and certificates

(vi)   details of when any instructions to be provided by the Contractor or by the Employer's Representative will be required, and any that are outstanding

(vii) details of when any Sub-Contract Works Items or other things to be provided by the Employer or the Contractor will be required and any that are outstanding

(viii) details of any Delay Events and Compensation Events relating to the Sub-Contract Works that have occurred during the period, or are unresolved

(ix)   details of any accidents, injuries, hazardous incidents, environmental incidents, labour relations problems and public relations problems arising in relation to or affecting the Sub-Contract Works

(x)   details of anything that might have an adverse effect on the execution of the Sub-Contract Works, the steps the NN Sub-Contractor is taking or proposed to take to reduce those risks, and any steps that the NN Sub-Contractor proposes that the Contractor or Employer should take to reduce those risks

(xi)   anything else that the NN Sub-Contractor considers relevant to a progress report

(xii) anything else relevant to a progress report that the Contractor reasonably directs.

(8)   If, provided reasonable notice has been given by the Contractor of the requirement for programme or progress report information, due to the Sub-Contractor's failure to submit such information to the Contractor in accordance with this clause, the Contractor suffers a payment reduction under clauses 4.9.3 or 11.4.2 of the Main Contract, the Contractor shall, subject to clause 11(b) hereof, be entitled to deduct the same amount from the next payment to the Sub-Contractor. To the extent that the deduction is partially caused by default of the Sub-Contractor, a fair and reasonable proportion of the sum withheld by the Employer shall be withheld from the Sub-Contractor.

NOTE

The NN Sub-Contractor's obligations in relation to programming and reporting are set out.

The NN Sub-Contractor shall carry out and complete the sub-contract works to meet the requirements of the Main Contract programme.

The NN Sub-Contractor shall liaise and co-operate with the Contractor and other Sub-Contractors and shall programme the sub-contract works so that the works are not delayed or disrupted.

The NN Sub-Contractor is required to provide relevant information in respect of programming and progress of the sub-contract works to enable the Contractor to meet its obligations under the Main Contract in relation to programme and progress reporting.

The NN Sub-Contractor must provide information for the Contractor's programme in relation to when they will require any instructions, works items or any other thing to be given by the Employer or the Contractor, a programme showing the order in which they propose to execute the works and the duration of the various activities, details of procurement, manufacture, delivery, construction, testing and commissioning of works items and the sequence and timing of inspections and tests, and for civil engineering works, the methods by which the NN Sub-Contractor proposes to execute the works and any temporary works.

The NN Sub-Contractor must co-operate with the Employer, the Employer's personnel or the Contractor in relation to preparation, monitoring and revision of the programme.

The NN Sub-Contractor must provide monthly progress reports within four working days after the end of the month to which it relates. It shall be in the format required by the Contractor to meet its obligation under the Main Contract. There are 12 headings listed in sub-clause 4(7) which should be included in the progress reports:

1. a detailed description of progress of each stage of the sub-contract works;

2. the names of off-site suppliers in relation to the sub-contract works, and the progress and location of the design, manufacture, fabrication, delivery, installation, testing and commissioning of sub-contract works items;

3. details of the NN Sub-Contractor's personnel and NN Sub-Contractor's "things on the site";

4. status of preparation and review of sub-contract documents;

5. copies of quality assurance documents and tests results and certificates;

6. details of when any instructions to be provided by the Contractor or by the Employer's Representative will be required, and any that are outstanding;

7. details of when any sub-contract works Items or other things to be provided by the Employer or the Contractor will be required and any that are outstanding;

8. details of any delay events and compensation events relating to the sub-contract works that have occurred during the period, or are unresolved;

9. details of any accidents, injuries, hazardous incidents, environmental incidents, labour relations problems and public relations problems arising in relation to or affecting the sub-contract works;

10. details of anything that might have an adverse effect on the execution of the sub-contract works, the steps the NN Sub-Contractor is taking or proposed to take to reduce those risks, and any steps that the NN Sub-Contractor proposes that the Contractor or Employer should take to reduce those risks;

11. anything else that the NN Sub-Contractor considers relevant to a progress report;

12. anything else relevant to a progress report that the Contractor reasonably directs.

Under the Main Contract if the Contractor fails to provide a revised programme within 15 working days of a request from when the Employer's Representative, then the Employer may deduct 15 percent of any payment due to the Contractor until the new programme is provided. Clause 4.8 of the NN sub-contract allows the main Contractor to pass on this penalty to the NN Sub-Contractor to the extent that the deduction is partially caused by default of the NN Sub-Contractor.

4(e)   Notice and Time for Contractors Obligations

(1) The NN Sub-Contractor shall give the Contractor at least 12 working days advance notice of the date by which the NN Sub-Contractor requires any instructions or any other thing that the Contractor is to provide.

(2) To the extent that the NN Sub-Contractor requires any instructions or other thing from the Contractor to enable it proceed with the Sub-Contract Works, the same will be provided by

the Contractor within a reasonable time. However, to the extent that such instructions or other thing are to be provided by the Employer or Employer's Representative to the Contractor under the Main Contract, the Contractor's only obligation to the NN Sub-Contractor will be to pass on such instructions or other thing to the NN Sub-Contractor within a reasonable time of receipt from the Employer or the Employer's Representative.

> **NOTE**
>
> The NN Sub-Contractor must provide 12 working days advance notice of the date by which instructions or work items or other things are required from the Contractor. This can be carried out when producing the programme and a full list provided to the Contractor when providing the programme. Any failure by the Contractor to provide the requested information on time, that causes a delay to the NN Sub-Contractor, will entitle the Sub-Contractor to an extension of time and costs.

4(f)   Meetings

The NN Sub-Contractor shall attend meetings with the Contractor and with the Employer's Representative or other relevant parties at such times and venues as the Contractor may reasonably require. If the NN Sub-Contractor is provided with minutes of any such meeting, the NN Sub-Contractor shall notify the Contractor of any objection to the minutes within 3 working days of receipt. Otherwise, unless clearly wrong, the minutes shall be considered correct.

> **NOTE**
>
> Regular meetings shall take place which the Sub-Contractor will be required to attend.

4(g)   Proposed Instructions

If any request is made by the Employer's Representative under clause 10.4 ("Proposed Instructions") of the Main Contract for proposals for a Proposed Instruction, the NN Sub-Contractor shall provide such calculations and information (including design details if appropriate) as is necessary for the Contractor to comply with that request in so far as the request relates to the Sub-Contract Works and will do so in sufficient time to enable the Contractor meet the time requirements of that provision.

> **NOTE**
>
> Under the Main Contract, the Contractor is required to submit proposed instructions that may be requested by the Employer's Representative. The NN Sub-Contractor must provide information as is necessary for the Contractor to comply with the request in so far as the request relates to the NN sub-contract works and will do so in sufficient time for the Contractor to comply with his obligations.

4(h)   NN Sub-Contractor's Things not to be removed

The NN Sub-Contractor shall submit details to the Contractor before removing any NN Sub-Contractor's Things from the Site prior to the issue by the Employer's Representative of the Certificate of Substantial Completion of the whole of the Works or of a Section of the Works.

> **NOTE**
>
> The Sub-Contractor must inform the Contractor before he removes any NN Sub-Contractor's things from site before substantial completion.

5. NN SUB-CONTRACTOR'S PERSONNEL

5(a) Liability

The NN Sub-Contractor is liable for the acts and omissions of NN Sub-Contractor Personnel [including any design carried out] as if they were the NN Sub-Contractor's own acts and omissions.

5(b) Qualifications and Competence

The NN Sub-Contractor shall ensure that the NN Sub-Contractor Personnel are suitably qualified and experienced and competent to carry out their respective tasks.

5(c) Pay and Conditions of Employment of NN Sub-Contractor's Personnel

(1) The provisions of clause 5.3 ("Pay and Conditions of Employment") of the Main Contract will apply, *mutatis mutandis*, to the NN Sub-Contractor in respect of the NN Sub-Contractor's Personnel.

(2) Sub-clause 5.3.3A(2) of the Main Contract shall only be included as a term of the Sub-Contract if the Schedule to the Main Contract Part 1J says so, and if not, neither sub-clause 5.3.3A(2) nor its omission shall be taken into account. In the event of 5.3.3A(2) applying, the NN Sub-Contractor will grant to the Employer and to the Contractor every facility and co-operation and will ensure that the NN Sub-Contractor's Personnel does likewise in that regard.

(3) If the NN Sub-Contractor has not complied with this clause 5(c), the Contractor shall (without limiting its other rights or remedies) be entitled to estimate the amount that should have been paid to work persons (and contributions that should have been made on their behalf), and the Contractor may deduct the estimated amount from any payment due to the NN Sub-Contractor, until the Contractor is satisfied that all proper amounts have been paid.

(4) The NN Sub-Contractor shall give to the Contractor with each NN Sub-Contractor's Interim Statement under clause 11(a), a certificate in respect of the work to which the Interim Statement relates to the effect that the NN Sub-Contractor and the NN Sub-Contractor's Personnel have complied in full with this clause 5(c). The certificate will be in similar form to that required of the Contractor under the terms of the Main Contract subject to such modifications as the Contractor may reasonably require.

NOTE

Under the Main Contract the Contractor shall ensure tat the rates of pay and conditions of employment of each work person comply with applicable law and are no less favourable than those for the relevant category of work person in any employment agreement registered under the Industrial Relations Acts 1946–2004. This speaks for itself. Under sub-clause 5(c) of the NN sub-contact this obligation is passed on to the NN Sub-Contractor.

Under the Main Contract to confirm compliance with this clause the Contractor has to provide the Employer's Representative with a certificate – Model Form 15 that the Contractor has complied in full with clause 5.3. The Contractor has to submit this certificate with each interim statement under clause 11.1 (Interim Payment) otherwise payment will be delayed. This requirement is passed on to the NN Sub-Contractor in the NN Sub-Contract.

5(d) Sub-Sub-Contractors

The NN Sub-Contractor shall not subcontract the Sub-Contract Works, in whole or in part, without the consent in writing of the Contractor.

5(e)   Collateral Warranties

If the Schedule to the Main Contract (part 1F) states that a collateral warranty is required from the NN Sub-Contractor, the NN Sub-Contractor shall provide to the Contractor a collateral warranty in the form included in the Works Requirements (or if there is none a form approved by the Employer) executed by the NN Sub-Contractor on or before the date it is required under the terms of the Main Contract. If the Employer makes any deduction from payments otherwise due to the Contractor under the terms of the Main Contract because any such collateral warranty has not been provided, the Contractor will be entitled, subject to clause 11(b) hereof, to withhold payment of the sum specified in the Main Contract Schedule Part 1 F from any sum due to the NN Sub-Contractor until the collateral warranty is provided.

5(f)   Removal of Work Persons

The NN Sub-Contractor shall remove from the site any NN Sub-Contractor Personnel where the Employer's Representative so directs under the terms of the Main Contract. The NN Sub-Contractor will also remove from the site any NN Sub-Contractor Personnel where the Contractor so directs because of the NN Sub-Contractor Personnel's negligence or incompetence or on the basis that the NN Sub-Contractor Personnel's presence on the site is not conducive to safety, health or good order.

6. PROPERTY

6(a) Ownership of Work Items and Infringement of Property Rights

The NN Sub-Contractor will ensure that in so far as sub-clauses 6.1 and 6.2 of the Main Contract relate to Sub-Contract Works Items, NN Sub-Contractor Things or otherwise relate to the Sub-Contract Works, that the Contractor is not in breach of those provisions.

> **NOTE**
>
> Work items means a part of the sub-contract works, or anything that the NN Sub-Contractor intends will become part of the works and temporary works for the works.

6(b) Works Requirements

The Works Requirements shall remain the property of the Employer and the NN Sub-Contractor shall not use them (and shall ensure that the NN Sub-Contractor's Personnel do not use them) for any purpose other than to perform the Sub-Contract or to prosecute or defend a dispute under the Sub-Contract.

6(c) Property and Rights in NN Sub-Contractor's Documents

The entitlements of the Employer in relation to the Contractor's Documents under clause 6.4 of the Main Contract will apply in relation to the Sub-Contract Documents and the obligations of the Contractor under that clause will apply *mutatis mutandis* to the NN Sub-Contractor in relation to the NN Sub-Contractor's Documents.

> **NOTE**
>
> Under the Main Contract the Employer can request ownership in relation to the Contractor's documents. This will apply to NN Sub-Contractor's documents and the obligations of the Contractor under clause 6.4 of the Main Contract will apply equally to the NN Sub-Contractor in relation to the NN Sub-Contract's documents.

7. THE SITE

7(a) Lands Made Available for the Works

The Contractor shall from time to time make available to the NN Sub-Contractor such part or parts of the Site and such means of access thereto within the Site as shall be necessary to enable the NN Sub-Contractor to execute the Sub-Contract Works in accordance with the NN Sub-Contract, but the Contractor shall not be bound to give the NN Sub-Contractor exclusive possession or exclusive control of any part of the Site, save as expressly provided for otherwise in the Sub-Contract Documents.

> **NOTE**
>
> The Contractor shall, from time to time, make available to the NN Sub-Contractor such part or parts of the site and such means of access thereto within the site as shall be necessary to enable the NN Sub-Contractor to execute the sub-contract works in accordance with the NN Sub-Contract, but the Contractor shall not be bound to give the NN Sub-Contractor exclusive possession or exclusive control of any part of the site, save as expressly provided for otherwise in the sub-contract documents.

7(b) Scaffolding

The Contractor shall permit the NN Sub-Contractor for the purpose of executing and completing the Sub-Contract Works to use such standing scaffolding as is from time to time provided by the Contractor in connection with the Works, but the Contractor shall not be bound to provide or retain such scaffolding for the NN Sub-Contractor's use unless otherwise stated in the Sub-Contract Documents.

7(c) Attendances

(1) The Contractor shall provide general attendances as stated in the Method of Measurement identified in the Appendix Part 1. Special attendances listed in the Appendix Part 1 will be provided by the Contractor. Otherwise the NN Sub-Contractor shall provide everything necessary for the execution of the Sub-Contract Works. The Contractor will provide all attendances required by this clause in a timely manner so as not to cause delay or disrupt progress of the Sub-Contract Works.

(2) The NN Sub-Contractor will be responsible for and bear the cost (to the extent that this cost is not recoverable as Compensation Event under the Main Contract) of removal from site and disposal of hazardous waste (as defined by Section 4(2)(a) of the Waste Act 1996) arising from the execution of the Sub-Contract Works.

7(d) Security and Safety of the Site and Nuisance

The NN Sub-Contractor will ensure that neither it nor the NN Sub-Contractor Personnel will cause the Contractor to be in breach of clause 7.5 ("Security and Safety of the Site and Nuisance") of the Main Contract.

7(e) Access and Traffic Control

The NN Sub-Contractor shall provide at its own cost for any necessary traffic control and access to the Sub-Contract Works, and shall take all reasonable steps to ensure that its traffic and that of the NN Sub-Contractor Personnel:-

(i) complies with the restrictions concerning laden weight and dimensions in the Law; and

(ii) does not damage roads (except for ordinary wear) bridges or other property.

7(f)   Setting Out The Works

Unless otherwise agreed between the parties, the NN Sub-Contractor will set out the Sub-Contract Works in compliance with clause 7.7 ("Setting Out the Works") of the Main Contract.

7(g)   Archaeological Objects and Human Remains

If any fossils, coins, antiquities, monuments or other items of value or of archaeological or geological interest or human remains are discovered on or adjacent to the Site, the NN Sub-Contractor shall not disturb them, but shall take all necessary steps to preserve them, and shall promptly notify the Contractor and comply with any instructions. As between the parties, these items shall be the Contractor's property.

7(h)   Condition of Site on Completion

At Substantial Completion of the Works or of any Section of the Works, of which the Sub-Contract Works form the whole or part, the NN Sub-Contractor shall remove from the Site (or section of the Site, as the case may be) the NN Sub-Contractor's Things not required to perform the NN Sub-Contractor's remaining obligations, and leave the Works or Section in an orderly manner. At the end of the Defects Period, the NN Sub-Contractor shall remove from the Site any remaining NN Sub-Contractor's Things.

7(i)   Working Times

The NN Sub-Contractor shall ensure that the NN Sub-Contractor's Personnel work on the Site only during the working times permitted under the terms of the Main Contract unless:-

(i)   there is imminent danger to safety or health or of damage to the Works or other property or

(ii) otherwise agreed with the Contractor.

8. QUALITY, TESTING AND DEFECTS

8(a) Standards of Workmanship and Works Items

The NN Sub-Contractor shall ensure all of the following:-

(1) that the Sub-Contract Works are designed (to the extent that this is the NN Sub-Contractor's responsibility), executed and completed:

    (i) in accordance with all the requirements in, and reasonably inferred from, the Main Contract, the Contractor's Documents, the Sub-Contract and the NN Sub-Contractor's Documents.

    (ii) In a proper and workmanlike manner and using good practice.

(2) that all Sub-Contract Works Items (whether or not the NN Sub-Contractor is required to select them):-

    (i) comply with the Sub-Contract and the Legal Requirements

    (ii) are (unless the Sub-Contract provides otherwise) new and of good quality

(3) that all materials and goods that are Sub-Contract Works Items are fit for their intended purpose in the Works

(4) that the completed Sub-Contract Works are fit for their intended purpose as stated in or to be inferred from the Works Requirements or from the Sub-Contract.

8(b) Quality Assurance

The NN Sub-Contractor shall establish and implement quality assurance procedures as required by the Main Contract Works Requirements in so far as they relate to the Sub-Contract Works, including procedures for establishing quality assurance systems for itself and any sub-sub-contractors. The quality assurance procedures shall be reflected in appropriate quality plans submitted to the Contractor. The NN Sub-Contractor shall give to the Contractor copies of all reports prepared in accordance with the NN Sub-Contractor quality assurance procedures. The Employer's Representative or the Contractor may monitor, spot check and audit the NN Sub-Contractor's quality assurance procedures and the NN Sub-Contractor will cooperate with the Employer's Representative and with the Contractor in the conduct of any such spot check.

> **NOTE**
>
> The NN Sub-Contractor shall establish and implement quality assurance requirements as required by the Main Contract Works requirements in so far as they relate to the sub-contract works, including procedures for establishing quality assurance systems for itself and any Sub-Sub-Contractors. The quality assurance procedures shall be reflected in appropriate quality plans that the NN Sub-Contractor submits to the Contractor. The quality assurance procedures shall be reflected in appropriate quality plans that the Contractor submits to the Employer's Representative. The Employer's Representative or the Contractor may monitor, carry out spot checks and audit the Contractor's quality assurance procedures.

8(c) Inspection and Tests

(1) The NN Sub-Contractor will have the same rights and obligations in relation to the Sub-Contract Works, *mutatis mutandis*, as the Contractor has under clause 8.3 ("Inspection") of the Main Contract in relation to the Works.

(2)   The NN Sub-Contractor will have the same rights and obligations in relation to the Sub-Contract Works, *mutatis mutandis*, as the Contractor has under clause 8.4 ("Tests") of the Main Contract in relation to the Works. The Employer's Representative, others authorised by the Employer and the Contractor may attend and observe the tests and the NN Sub-Contractor shall facilitate such attendance and observation.

8(d)   Defects

(1)   The Contractor may direct the NN Sub-Contractor to search for a Defect or suspected Defect or its cause. This may include uncovering, dismantling, re-covering and re-erecting work, providing facilities for tests, testing and inspecting. If, through searching or otherwise, the NN Sub-Contractor discovers a Defect, the NN Sub-Contractor shall notify the Contractor as soon as practicable.

(2)   If, through notification or otherwise, the Contractor becomes aware of a Defect, the Contractor may direct the NN Sub-Contractor to do any or all of the following:-

    (i)   to remove the defective Sub-Contract Works Item from the Site

    (ii)   to demolish the defective Sub-Contract Works Item, if incorporated in the Works.

    (iii) to reconstruct, replace or correct the defective Sub-Contract Works Item

    (vi)   not to deliver the defective Sub-Contract Works Item to the Site

(3)   The NN Sub-Contractor shall comply with any direction under this sub-clause 8(d) within the reasonable times (if any) the Contractor directs and in any event within any time limit imposed by the Employer's Representative. If the NN Sub-Contractor fails to begin the work required to comply with the direction within the reasonable time directed (if any) or fails to complete it as soon as practicable, the Contractor may have the work done by others and the NN Sub-Contractor shall on request pay the Contractor the cost thereby incurred.

(4)   Alternatively, the Contractor and the Employer's Representative may, with the Employer's and NN Sub-Contractor's agreement, agree that the Employer will accept the Defect, either in whole or subject to any change to the Works Requirements that the Employer's Representative directs. In this case, the Sub-Contract Sum shall be reduced by the amount that, in the opinion of the Employer's Representative, is the resulting decrease in the value of the Works to the Employer. If the Contractor notifies the NN Sub-Contractor that the Employer will not accept a Defect, this shall be conclusive. Notwithstanding this provision, the NN Sub-Contractor shall be entitled in any case to make good any Defect in the Sub-Contract Works and thus avoid a deduction from the Sub-Contract Sum in respect of the Defect.

(5)   If a Defect in the Sub-Contract Works deprives the Employer of substantially the whole benefit of the Works or any Section or other material part of the Works, the Employer's Representative may reject the Works or the relevant part of the Works. In this event, the NN Sub-Contractor will indemnify the Contractor in relation to any loss incurred by the Contractor under clause 8.5 ("Defects") of the Main Contract or otherwise.

8(e)   Defects Period & Defects Certificate

(1)   As soon as practicable, the NN Sub-Contractor shall complete any outstanding works and rectify any Defects brought to his attention by the Contractor either prior to Substantial Completion or during the Defects Period. In so doing, and in conducting any tests after Substantial Completion, the NN Sub-Contractor shall cause as little disruption as possible to occupants and users of the Works.

(2)   The NN Sub-Contractor will indemnify the Contractor in relation to any reduction to the Contract Sum made under clause 8.5 ("Defects") of the Main Contract in so far as that reduction relates to a Defect in the Sub-Contract Works.

(3) Nothing in this clause nor any exercise or non-exercise by the Employer, the Employer's Representative or the Contractor of their rights under this clause 8(e), nor the Defects Certificate, relieves the NN Sub-Contractor of any obligation in relation to any Defect in the Sub-Contract Works, except to the extent that a Defect is accepted by agreement under sub-clause 8(d)(4) hereof.

9.   TIME AND COMPLETION

9(a)   Starting Date

The Sub-Contractor shall commence work on site within ten working days, or such other period as may be entered in the Appendix Part 1, of receipt of the Contractor's written instructions so to do and shall thereafter proceed with due diligence with the execution and completion of the Sub-Contract Works.

9(b)   Suspension

(1)   The Contractor may instruct the NN Sub-Contractor to suspend all or part of the Sub-Contract Works if the Contractor has been instructed to suspend work by the Employer / Employer's Representative or the Contractor has suspended the Works by reason of not being paid by the Employer. The NN Sub-Contractor shall comply with the instruction and, during the suspension, shall protect, store and secure the affected Sub-Contract Works Items against deterioration, loss and damage and maintain the Sub-Contract Insurances. The NN Sub-Contractor shall take all reasonable steps to mitigate any loss suffered as a consequence of the suspension.

(2)   The Contractor will have no liability to the NN Sub-Contractor for any loss or delay suffered by the NN Sub-Contractor by reason of any such suspension except to the extent that the Contractor actually recovers payment from the Employer in relation thereto. If payment is made by the Employer to the Contractor in relation to losses sustained by reason of such suspension in relation thereto, the NN Sub-Contractor will be entitled to such proportion thereof as is fair and reasonable in all the circumstances.

> **NOTE**
>
> The Contractor may request the NN Sub-Contractor to suspend the works. In the event of a suspension the works have to be protected, stored and kept secure. The works will be resumed on instruction from the Contractor. The NN Sub-Contractor is entitled to the cost of any remedial works. The NN Sub-Contractor is entitled to an adjustment of the sub-contract sum and an extension of time.

9(c)   Notification of Delay

If the NN Sub-Contractor becomes aware or should have become aware that the Sub-Contract Works are being or are likely to be delayed for any reason, it shall notify the Contractor of the delay and its cause as soon as practicable but in any event within ten working days. Within a further 20 working days the NN Sub-Contractor shall give the Contractor full details of the delay in writing and its effect on the progress of the Sub-Contract Works. The NN Sub-Contractor will promptly provide any further information in relation to the delay which either the Contractor or the Employer's Representative requests.

> **NOTE**
>
> The NN Sub-Contractor shall, as soon as he becomes aware, or should have become aware that the NN sub-contract works are being, or are likely to be, delayed, he must notify the Contractor of the delay and the cause, as soon as practicable, but in any event within 10 working days. Within a further 20 working days the NN Sub-Contractor shall provide full details of the delay and the effect on progress of the works. The NN Sub-Contractor shall promptly provide any further information in relation to the delay as may be requested by the Contractor or the Employer's Representative. Notice of delays can be time-barred if they are not issued within the stated period.
>
> The time restraints i.e. 10 working days after the NN Sub-Contractor became aware of the delay and a further 20 working days to provide full details must be strictly adhered to.

9(d)   Programme Contingency

(1)   In this clause, references to the first threshold and second threshold are to the first and second threshold periods set out in the Schedule Part 1 K to the Main Contract.

(2)   The NN Sub-Contractor has included in the Initial Sub-Contract Sum a contingency for unrecovered costs incurred due to delays in completing the Sub-Contract Works caused by Compensation Events.

(3)   If the total number of Site Working Days required for the completion of the Sub-Contract Works is increased as a result of Compensation Events by a number of days which is less than or equal to the first threshold, the NN Sub-Contractor will not be entitled to any compensation for such delay.

(4)   If the total number of Site Working Days' required for the completion of the Subcontract Works is increased as a result of Compensation Events by a number of days which exceeds the first threshold, compensation shall be payable in respect of that number of Site Working Days delay less:

(i)   the number of Site Working Days stated as the first threshold; and less

(ii)   half the number of Site Working Days delay caused by the Compensation Events after deducting the first threshold, but the total deduction under this sub-paragraph (ii) shall not exceed the second threshold.

[For example, if the first threshold is 20 Site Working Days, and the second threshold is 30 Site Working Days:-

- If the NN Sub-Contractor suffers a delay of 28 Site Working Days due to Compensation Events, the Compensation payable would be for 4 Site Working Days, calculated as follows:

$$28 - 20 - (28 - 20) \div 2 = 4.$$

- If the NN Sub-Contractor suffers a delay of 90 Site Working Days due to Compensation Events, Compensation would be payable in respect of 40 Site Working Days, calculated as follows:-

$$90 - 20 - 30 = 40.$$

In this case, the deduction under sub-paragraph (ii) would have been

$$(90 - 20) \div 2 = 35.$$

but this is higher than the second threshold, so the second threshold (30) is substituted].

(5)   If the Main Contract is the public works contract for minor civil engineering and building works sub-paragraphs (1) and (4) of this sub-clause shall not apply and the reference in sub-paragraph (3) to the first threshold will be construed as referring to the threshold period provided for at sub-clause 9.4.2 of the Main Contract. In those circumstances, if the number of Site Working Days required for the completion of the Sub-Contract Works is increased as a result of Compensation Events by a number of days which is in excess of that threshold, the NN Sub-Contractor will be entitled to be compensated, as provided herein, only for the Site Working Days in excess of the threshold.

NOTE

The contingency for delays has to be built into the programme. There are two "Thresholds". The amount of the contingency will be given to the NN Sub-Contractor in the Schedule, Part 1 K of the Main Contract document at tender stage. Before an extension of time is granted the days in the first threshold must be exceeded, then the contingency in the second threshold only entitles the Contractor to 50 percent of those delays. The example in clause 9(d)(4) shows how the extensions of time are calculated.

10. CLAIMS AND ADJUSTMENTS

10(a) Notification and Procedure

(1) If the NN Sub-Contractor considers that it is entitled to an adjustment to the Sub-Contract Sum or that it has any other entitlement under or in relation to the Sub-Contract (including damages for breach of contract on the part of the Contractor), the NN Sub-Contractor shall, as soon as practicable and in any event within 10 working days after it became aware or should have become aware of such entitlement, give notice of this to the Contractor. The notice must prominently state that it is being given under this sub-clause 10(a)(1). Within a further 20 working days after giving the notice, the NN Sub-Contractor will give to the Contractor details of the following:-

    (i) all relevant facts about the claim

    (ii) a detailed calculation and (so far as practicable) a proposal, based on that calculation, of any adjustment to be made to the Sub-Contract Sum and of the amount of any other entitlement claimed by the NN Sub-Contractor

    (iii) if the total number of Site Working Days required for completion of the Sub-Contract works is increased by the delay, full details of the extent of the delay and the effect it is likely to have on the completion of the Sub-Contract works.

(2) The NN Sub-Contractor shall provide any further information requested by the Contractor in relation to the event or circumstance.

(3) If the NN Sub-Contractor does not give notice and details in accordance with and within the time provided in sub-clause 10(a)(1) notwithstanding anything else in the Sub-Contract the NN Sub-Contractor shall not be entitled to an increase to the Sub-Contract Sum and the Contractor shall be released from all liability to the NN Sub-Contractor in relation to the matter, except to the extent that the Contractor recovers additional payment from the Employer in respect of the Sub-Contract Works notwithstanding the failure of the NN Sub-Contractor to give such notice, in which case the NN Sub-Contractor will be entitled to corresponding payment valued in accordance with the Sub-Contract.

(4) If the cause of the claim has a continuing effect, the NN Sub-Contractor shall update the above information at monthly intervals.

(5) The NN Sub-Contractor shall keep detailed contemporary records to substantiate any aspect of an event or circumstance in relation to which it has, or is entitled to, give notice under this sub-clause 10(a) and its resulting costs. These shall include any records the Contractor directs the NN Sub-Contractor to keep. The NN Sub-Contractor shall provide the records to the Contractor if so directed.

NOTE

If the NN Sub-Contractor considers that there should be an extension of time or an adjustment to the contract sum he shall provide such notice to the Contractor within 10 working days after becoming or should have been aware of something that would give rise to an entitlement. The notice must prominently state that it is being given under sub-clause 10(a)(1).

Within a further 20 working days after giving the notice, the NN Sub-Contractor shall provide:

  i) All relevant facts;

  ii) A detailed calculation and a proposal based on the calculation of the adjustment to be made to the contract sum and of the amount of any other entitlement claimed by the NN Sub-Contractor.

The NN Sub-Contractor shall provide any further information requested by the Contractor in relation to the matter.

If the NN Sub-Contractor does not comply with notices, details and time scales, then the NN Sub-Contractor shall not be entitled to an increase in the contract sum and the Contractor shall be released from all liability to the NN Sub-Contractor in relation to the matter. Sub-clause 10(5) requires the NN Sub-Contractor to keep contemporary records of all events under 10(a). The Contractor may instruct the NN Sub-Contractor to keep records.

10(b)   Adjustments to the Sub-Contract Sum

(1)   Adjustments to the Sub-Contract Sum may arise in respect of additional work, substituted work or omitted work as a consequence of a Compensation Event (as defined in the Schedule Part 1 K of the Main Contract) or as a consequence of complying with an instruction from the Contractor in relation to a matter which could not reasonably have been anticipated by the NN Sub-Contractor at the time of tendering.

(2)   If the additional work, substituted work or omitted work is the same as or similar to work for which there are rates in the NN Sub-Contractor's tender and is to be executed under similar conditions, the adjustment of the Sub-Contract Sum shall be determined using those rates

(3)   If the additional work, substituted work or omitted work is not similar to work for which there are rates in the NN Sub-Contractor's tender and is not to be executed under similar conditions, the adjustment of the Sub-Contract Sum shall be determined on the basis of the rates in the NN Sub-Contractor's tender when that is reasonable

(4)   If the adjustment can not be determined under the above rules, the Contractor shall make a fair valuation

(5)   The Contractor may direct that adjustment to the Sub-Contract Sum in respect of additional work or substituted work will be determined on the basis of the cost of performing the additional or substituted work, compared with the NN Sub-Contractor's cost without the Compensation Event or Contractor's instruction (as the case may be), as follows:-

   (i)   The number of hours worked or to be worked by each category of work person stated in the Appendix Part 2 and engaged on the work to which the Compensation Event or Contractor's Instruction (as the case may be) relates, on or off the Site, multiplied in each case by the tendered hourly rate for that category stated in the Appendix Part 2.

   (ii)   The cost of materials used in that work, taking into account discounts and excluding VAT, plus the percentage adjustment tendered by the NN Sub-Contractor and stated in the Appendix Part 2

   (iii)   The cost of plant reasonably used for that work whether hired or owned by the NN Sub-Contractor, at the rates in the document listed in the Schedule Part 1 K of the Main Contract plus or minus the percentage adjustment tendered by the NN Sub-Contractor and stated in the Appendix Part 2. If the document listed in the Schedule to the Main Contract does not give a rate for a plant item, a market rental rate shall be used, plus or minus the percentage adjustment.

   (iv)   The cost of design (if any) at the tendered rate. If the Sub-Contract Documents include a Pricing Document, the cost of design will be ascertained by reference to that document.

(6)   Where the adjustment to the Sub-Contract Sum arises as a consequence of a Compensation Event, the method of its determination shall correspond to that being applied by the Employer's Representative under Clause 10.6 of the Main Contract, unless otherwise agreed between the Contractor and the NN Sub-Contractor.

(7) Adjustments for delay cost shall be in accordance with sub-clause 10 (c) below

> **NOTE**
>
> The adjustment to the contract sum for a compensation event follows the traditional contract forms i.e. using rates contained in the pricing document, fair rates or recorded hours by the rates stated in the Appendix Part 2, together with the cost of plant and materials with the percentage additions quoted in the Appendix Part 2.

10(c) Delay Cost

(1) To the extent that the NN Sub-Contractor is delayed or incurs loss by reason of a Compensation Event, subject to clauses 10(a) and 9(d) hereof, the NN Sub-Contractor will be entitled to be compensated.

(2) To the extent that the NN Sub-Contractor incurs delay or loss by reason of any event other than as provided for in sub-clauses 10(c)(1) or 1(g), the NN Sub-Contractor will have no entitlement to be compensated.

(3) If a delay has more than one cause, and one or more of the causes is not an event for which there is an entitlement to additional payment or recovery of costs incurred, there shall be no increase to the Sub-Contract Sum in respect of the delay cost for the period of concurrent delay.

(4) To the extent that the NN Sub-Contractor is entitled to compensation for delay caused by Compensation Events under sub-clause 10(c)(1), there shall be added to the Sub-Contract Sum for each Site Working Day for which compensation is payable (calculated in accordance with clause 9(d) above) either of the following (depending on which option has been selected in the Schedule to the Main Contract Part 1 K):-

   (i) the daily rate of delay cost tendered by the NN Sub-Contractor in the Appendix Part 2 hereto, or

   (ii) the expenses (excluding profit and loss of profit) unavoidably incurred by the NN Sub-Contractor as a result of the delay caused by the Compensation Event.

> **NOTE**
>
> To the extent that the NN Sub-Contractor is delayed or incurs loss by reason of a compensation event, the NN Sub-Contractor will be entitled to be compensated.
>
> If the Contractor causes delay or additional cost to the NN Sub-Contractor, the NN Sub-Contractor will be entitled to be compensated by the Contractor for the reasonable loss incurred. Delay costs are added as defined in the Appendix Part 2. All the costs are capped to that stated in the Appendix Part 2.

10(d) Price Variation

Whichever of clauses PV1 or PV2 has been selected in the Schedule Part 1M of the Main Contract shall apply to the Sub-Contract mutatis mutandis.

> **NOTE**
>
> Whichever of clauses PV1 or PV2 has been selected in the Schedule, Part 1 M of the Main Contract shall apply to the sub-contract equally.

11. PAYMENT

11(a) Interim Statements

(1) The Contractor shall advise the NN Sub-Contractor of dates on which it will submit Contractor's Interim Statements in accordance with clause 11.1 ("Interim Payment") of the Main Contract.

(2) Not later than 7 working days before each date for submission of a Contractor's Interim Statement, the NN Sub-Contractor shall submit to the Contractor a statement (the **NN Sub-Contractor's Interim Statement**) including a detailed breakdown of the sum it considers to be the value of the Sub-Contract Works completed up to the end of that period and indicating the amount it considers payable in respect of that period, which amount will be calculated as follows:-

   (i) the cumulative value of the Sub-Contract Works properly designed (to the extent that this is the NN Sub-Contractor's responsibility) and executed, valued in accordance with the rates and prices used in the calculation of the Sub-Contract Sum, plus

   (ii) where the NN Sub-Contractor is required to carry out design of the Sub-Contract Works, the value of design completed to date, plus

   (iii) if applicable [as provided for below in sub-clause 11(e)] the value of unfixed Sub-Contract Works Items, plus

   (iv) amounts due by the Contractor in respect of Compensation Events under the Main Contract as provided for in clause 10 hereof, plus

   (v) other sums claimed by the NN Sub-Contractor in accordance with clause 10 hereof, plus

   (vi) Other adjustments in accordance with Clause 10 hereof, plus

   (vii) If applicable, any sum payable in relation to price variation under clause 10(d) hereof, less

   (viii) retention in accordance with this clause, less

   (ix) the total amount of previous payments

(3) The NN Sub-Contractor's Interim Statements shall be accompanied by sufficient information in relation to progress of the Sub-Contract Works, together with any other supporting evidence required by the Employer's Representative (of which the Contractor will give reasonable notice to the NN Sub-Contractor), to enable the Contractor to meet the requirements of clause 11.1 ("Interim Payment") of the Main Contract.

(4) The NN Sub-Contractor will provide with each of the NN Sub-Contractor's Interim Statements the certificate required by clause 5(c)(4) (Pay and Conditions of Employment of NN Sub-Contractor's Personnel) hereof. The provision of this certificate is a condition precedent to payment by the Contractor to the NN Sub-Contractor in respect of that period.

(5) If the NN Sub-Contractor fails to submit an Interim Statement as and at the time required, the Contractor may include in its Interim Statement its own estimate of the sum due in respect of the Sub-Contract Works but shall not be obliged to do so. In this event, any payment to the NN Sub-Contractor will be based on that estimate and will be subject to the NN Sub-Contractor providing an Interim Statement showing that at least this amount is due and providing the certificate (in respect of Pay and Conditions of Employment) required by clause 5(c)(4) hereof.

NOTE

The Contractor shall advise the NN Sub-Contractor of dates on which it will submit Contractor's Interim Statements in accordance with clause 11.1 ("Interim Payment") of the Main Contract. Not later than seven working days before each date for submission of a Contractor's Interim Statement, the NN Sub-Contractor shall submit to the Contractor a statement (the "NN Sub-Contractor's Interim Statement") including a detailed breakdown of the sum it considers to be the value of the Sub-Contract Works completed up to the end of that period and indicating the amount it considers payable in respect of that period, which amount will be calculated as follows:

1. the cumulative value of the Sub-Contract Works properly designed (to the extent that this is the NN Sub-Contractor's responsibility) and executed, valued in accordance with the rates and prices used in the calculation of the Sub-Contract Sum, plus

2. the value of design completed to date, plus

3. the value of unfixed Sub-Contract Works Items, plus

4. amounts due by the Contractor in respect of Compensation Events under the Main Contract as provided for in clause 10 hereof, plus

5. other sums claimed by the NN Sub-Contractor, plus

6. other adjustments, plus

7. any sum payable in relation to price variation under clause 10(d) hereof, less

8. retention in accordance with this clause, less

9. the total amount of previous payments

The NN Sub-Contractor's Interim Statements shall be accompanied by sufficient information in relation to progress of the Sub-Contract Works, together with any other supporting evidence required by the Employer's Representative (of which the Contractor will give reasonable notice to the NN Sub-Contractor), to enable the Contractor to meet the requirements of clause 11.1 ("Interim Payment") of the Main Contract.

The NN Sub-Contractor will provide with each of the NN Sub-Contractor's Interim Statements the certificate required by clause 5(c)(4) (Pay and Conditions of Employment of NN Sub-Contractor's Personnel). The provision of this certificate is a condition precedent to payment by the Contractor to the NN Sub-Contractor in respect of that period.

If the NN Sub-Contractor fails to submit an Interim Statement as and at the time required, the Contractor may include in its Interim Statement its own estimate of the sum due in respect of the Sub-Contract Works, but shall not be obliged to do so. In this event, any payment to the NN Sub-Contractor will be based on that estimate and will be subject to the NN Sub-Contractor providing an Interim Statement showing that at least this amount is due and providing the certificate (in respect of Pay and Conditions of Employment) required by clause 5(c)(4).

11(b)   Deductions

(1)   The Contractor may make equivalent pro-rata deductions from sums otherwise due to the NN Sub-Contractor as the Employer may make from sums due to the Contractor under clause 11.4 ("Full Payment") of the Main Contract, to the extent that the Contractor's default arises from a failure on the part of the NN Sub-Contractor to abide by the terms of this Sub-Contract. The Contractor shall notify the NN Sub-Contractor of the deduction, on or before the date the NN Sub-Contractor is due to be paid, giving particulars of how it arises and of its computation.

(2)   If the Employer's Representative in any certificate, issued in accordance with Clause 11.1.3 of the Main Contract, makes a reduction in the quantity of any item which is part of the Sub-Contract Works, the Contractor may make a corresponding reduction in the sum due to the

NN Sub-Contractor, provided the reduction by the Employer's Representative was not caused by the Contractor's negligence or breach of contract. The Contractor shall notify the NN Sub-Contractor of any such deduction, on or before the date the NN Sub-Contractor is due to be paid, giving full particulars of how the reduction in the sum due has been calculated.

(3)   If the Employer's Representative in any certificate, issued in accordance with Clause 11.1.3 of the Main Contract, makes a deduction in the sum claimed by the Contractor for the Sub-Contract Works in respect of any Compensation Event, the Contractor may make a corresponding deduction in the sum due to the NN Sub-Contractor. The Contractor shall notify the NN Sub-Contractor of any such deduction, on or before the date the NN Sub-Contractor is due to be paid, giving full particulars of how the deduction in the sum due has been calculated.

(4)   The Contractor may deduct from any sum otherwise due to the NN Sub-Contractor any sum to which the Contractor is entitled by reason of contra-charge in respect of this Sub-Contract or arising as a consequence of any breach by the NN Sub-Contractor of the terms of this Sub-Contract. The Contractor shall notify the NN Sub-Contractor of any deduction [other than deductions covered by sub-clauses 11(b)(1), (2) and (3) above] not later than 20 working days after the date for submission of the Contractor's Interim Statement under clause 11(a)(1) hereof, giving the reasons for it. The Contractor shall reasonably take into account any representations by the NN Sub-Contractor in respect of any deductions from interim payments.

(5)   The Contractor will not be entitled to make any deduction unless the NN Sub-Contractor has first been notified in accordance with sub-clauses (1), (2), (3) and (4) of this sub-clause.

NOTE

The Contractor may make deductions from sums due to the NN Sub-Contractor as the Employer may make from sums due to the Contractor under clause 11.4 ("Full Payment") of the Main Contract, to the extent that the Contractor's default arises from a failure on the part of the NN Sub-Contractor to abide by the terms of this Sub-Contract. The Contractor must notify the NN Sub-Contractor of the deduction before it is made by the Contractor.

11(c)   Interim Payments

(1)   The Contractor shall make each interim payment of the sum due to the NN Sub-Contractor not later than 20 working days after the issue by the Employer's Representative of each certificate in accordance with Clause 11.1.3 of the Main Contract. If the sum paid by the Contractor to the NN Sub-Contractor is less than shown on the NN Sub-Contractor's Interim Statement the Contractor, shall, at the time of making payment, provide to the NN Sub-Contractor a statement showing how the sum paid has been computed. In the event that the sum properly deductible by the Contractor exceeds the sum which would otherwise be payable to the NN Sub-Contractor, there shall be a debt due from the NN Sub-Contractor to the Contractor which shall be payable by the NN Sub-Contractor within 7 working days of either the date when payment would otherwise have been due to the NN Sub-Contractor or of the notification by the Contractor of the debt, whichever is the later.

(2)   If, due to default by the Contractor, payment to the NN Sub-Contractor is delayed beyond the time limit in sub-clause 11 (c) (1) above, the NN Sub-Contractor will be entitled to be paid interest for the period of the delay at the rate applicable under S.I. No.388 of 2002 European Communities (Late Payment in Commercial Transactions) Regulations 2002.

(3)   The Contractor shall, on request and without delay, advise the NN Sub-Contractor (providing substantiating documentation) of the dates when the Contractor's interim statements were actually submitted to the Employer's Representative in accordance with Clause 11.1.1 of the Main Contract and the dates on which the Contractor received certificates (for payment) issued by the Employer's Representative in accordance with Clause 11.1.3 of the Main Contract.

(4)   In the event that, because the amount due to the Contractor is less than the minimum stated in the Schedule Part 1 L of the Main Contract, no payment certificate is issued by the Employer's Representative for any particular period, the Contractor shall so advise the NN Sub-Contractor and shall pay the NN Sub-Contractor the sum due to it not later than 32 working days after the date the Contractor would otherwise have been due to submit its Interim Statement to the Employer.

> **NOTE**
>
> The Contractor shall make each interim payment of the sum due to the NN Sub-Contractor not later than 20 working days after the issue by the Employer's Representative of each certificate.
>
> The Contractor shall advise the NN Sub-Contractor of the dates when the Contractor's Interim Statements were actually submitted to the Employer's Representative and the dates on which the Contractor received certificates (for payment) issued by the Employer's Representative.
>
> In the event that, because the amount due to the Contractor is less than the minimum stated in the Schedule, Part 1 L of the Main Contract, no payment certificate is issued by the Employer's Representative for any particular period, the Contractor shall so advise the NN Sub-Contractor and shall pay the NN Sub-Contractor the sum due to it not later than 32 working days after the date the Contractor would otherwise have been due to submit its Interim Statement to the Employer.

11(d)   Enforcement

(1)   The NN Sub-Contractor shall not take steps to enforce payment of any sum due until 30 working days after the issue [or deemed issue under clause 11(d)(3) hereof] by the Employer's Representative of a certificate under Clause 11.1.3 of the Main Contract or, in the event that Clause 11(c)(4) applies, within 50 working days after the due date for submission of the Contractor's Interim Statement under the Main Contract unless:-

   i)   The Sub-Contract is terminated

   ii)   the Contractor has suspended work

   iii)   the Main Contract has been terminated

(2)   If any of the above sub-paragraphs (i) to (iii) applies, the NN Sub-Contractor may suspend work immediately and take action to recover the sum due. Otherwise, if the NN Sub-Contractor has not received payment of the sum due within the period stipulated in sub-clause 11(d)(1) above, the NN Sub-Contractor may:-

   i)   notify the Contractor of its intention to suspend the Sub-Contract Works

   ii)   not less than 15 working days later, if payment has still not been received, suspend the Sub-Contract Works

   iii)   if after a further 15 working days payment has still not been received, terminate the Sub-Contract

   In the event that the NN Sub-Contractor justifiably suspends the Sub-Contract Works because of non-payment by the Contractor of monies due, the consequent delay will be deemed to have been caused by the Contractor's breach.

(3)   If, after receiving a request from the NN Sub-Contractor under clause 11(c)(3) hereof, the Contractor fails to furnish information as to whether and when the Employer's Representative has issued a certificate (for payment) in accordance with clause 11.1.3 of the Main Contract, a certificate will be deemed to have been issued 20 working days after the due date for submission of the Contractor's Statement under clause 11.1 of the Main Contract. However the certificate will not be deemed to have been issued if the Contractor establishes to the reasonable satisfaction of the NN Sub-Contractor that such a certificate has not been issued and that this was not due to default or breach of contract on the part of the Contractor.

NOTE

The NN Sub-Contractor shall not take steps to enforce payment of any sum due until 30 working days after the issue or deemed issue by the Employer's Representative of a certificate under Clause 11.1.3 of the Main Contract or, in the event that Clause 11(c)(4) applies, within 50 working days after the due date for submission of the Contractor's Interim Statement under the Main Contract unless:

1. the Sub-Contract is terminated;

2. the Contractor has suspended work;

3. the Main Contract has been terminated.

If any of the above applies, the NN Sub-Contractor may suspend work immediately and take action to recover the sum due. Otherwise, if the NN Sub-Contractor has not received payment of the sum due within the period stipulated above, the NN Sub-Contractor may:

1. notify the Contractor of its intention to suspend the Sub-Contract Works;

2. not less than 15 working days later, suspend the Sub-Contract Works;

3. if after a further 15 working days, terminate the Sub-Contract.

11(e) Payment for Unfixed Works Items

The NN Sub-Contractor will be entitled to seek payment for unfixed Sub-Contract Work Items if payment for them may be claimed under the Main Contract. Payment will be subject to full compliance by the NN Sub-Contractor with the provisions of clause 11.2 ("Unfixed Works Items") of the Main Contract and to the title vesting in the Employer to the NN Sub-Contractor's Unfixed Work Items. The NN Sub-Contractor's entitlement to payment will be dependent upon the Employer's Representative including for such payment in a certificate for payment issued under the Main Contract. In the case of Work Items not delivered to the site, the NN Sub-Contractor will provide a bond for the benefit of the Contractor equivalent to that required by the Employer under clause 11.2 (2) (f) of the Main Contract and the NN Sub-Contractor will also bear the reasonable cost incurred by the Contractor in providing such a bond for the Employer, or if the bond relates only in part to Sub-Contract Work Items, the NN Sub-Contractor will bear a reasonable proportion of that cost.

NOTE

Under the Main Contract the Contractor can be paid for unfixed works items up to a value of 90 percent provided the contract allows such a provision which will be detailed in Part 1 L of the Schedule, provided:

• they have been completed and they are substantially ready to be incorporated in the works;

• title to them has been vested in the Employer;

• they are stored suitably on site.

These provisions are afforded to the NN Sub-Contractor under the NN Sub-Contract.
Payment for goods not delivered to site is provided for as follows:

• They have been completed and they are substantially ready to be incorporated in the works;

• Title to them has been vested in the Employer;

• They are stored suitably and marked to show they are the property of the Employer and that their destination is the site;

• They are clearly identified in a list provided to the Employer's Representative and with documentary evidence that title is vested in the Employer;

- They are insured as required by the contract and will be insured while in transit;

- The Employer is provided with a bond by a surety approved by the Employer's Representative for the amount to be paid.

11(f)　Retention

(i)　Retention will be deducted from all interim sums due to the Sub-contractor at the rate stated in the Schedule to the Main Contract (Part 1L). 20 working days after the issue by the Employer's Representative of the Certificate of Substantial Completion, half the sum so deducted will be payable to the NN Sub-Contractor and the remaining half (the second moiety) will be payable 20 working days after the issue by the Employer's Representative of the Defects Certificate. If, within 10 working days of the issue of the Certificate of Substantial Completion of the Works (or another date agreed between the Contractor and the NN Sub-Contractor) the NN Sub-Contractor provides to the Contractor a retention bond in or equivalent to the form incorporated in the Main Contract Works Requirements or, if there is none, a form approved by the Contractor (which approval is not to be unreasonably withheld) for the amount of the second moiety of retention and executed by a surety approved by the Contractor (approval not to be unreasonably withheld), the NN Sub-Contractor shall be entitled to be paid the second moiety.

(ii)　If by reason of the Employer's Representative issuing a Certificate of Substantial Completion for a Section of the Works, the Contractor becomes entitled to the release of the retention relating to the Sub-Contract Works earlier than would otherwise be the case, the Contractor shall pay to the NN Sub-Contractor the sum due by way of released retention in respect of the Sub-Contract within 20 working days of the date of the said Certificate of Substantial Completion.

11(g)　Final Statement

The NN Sub-Contractor shall submit to the Contractor its Final Statement of all sums due to the NN Sub-Contractor under the Sub-Contract, computed in the manner prescribed in sub-clause 11(a)(2) hereof, not later than five weeks after the date of the Certificate of Substantial Completion of the Works issued by the Employer's Representative (which date is to be promptly advised to the NN Sub-Contractor by the Contractor). [This shall not preclude the NN Sub-Contractor from submitting its Final Statement at an earlier date if it considers the Sub-Contract Works are complete]. If the NN Sub-Contractor fails to provide its Final Statement, the Contractor will make its own estimate of the final value of the Sub-Contract Works and the final payment due to the NN Sub-Contractor will be based on that estimate irrespective of whether the NN Sub-Contractor considers that estimate was too low.

NOTE

Within five weeks after substantial completion is certified, the NN Sub-Contractor shall provide a Final Statement which shall include all money that the NN Sub-Contractor considers due from the Contractor. The Contractor shall have no liability to the NN Sub-Contractor for any matter not detailed in the Final Statement except for indemnities or compensation events occurring after Substantial Completion was certified.

11(h)　Additional Work instructed after Substantial Completion

(1)　If, after the date of Substantial Completion has been certified, the Contractor instructs the NN Sub-Contractor to carry out additional work, either as a consequence of a Compensation Event under the Main Contract or otherwise, in order to obtain payment for it the NN Sub-Contractor will submit a supplemental account not later than one month after the end of the Defects Period (defined in the Schedule Part 1I of the Main Contract). Payment for this additional work will be included in the final payment to the NN Sub-Contractor or, in the event that no other payment is due to the NN Sub-Contractor, payment for the additional work will be not later than four months after the date of the Defects Certificate issued by the Employer's Representative.

(2)   The Contractor shall have no liability to the NN Sub-Contractor under or in relation to the Sub-Contract for any matter not detailed in the NN Sub-Contractor's Final Statement except in respect of additional work arising from an instruction from the Contractor issued after Substantial Completion of the Works was certified.

11(i)   Penultimate Payment

(1)   The Employer's Representative is required, by the Main Contract, to issue the Penultimate Payment Certificate within five months of the date of Substantial Completion of the Works. Within 20 working days of the issue by the Employer's Representative of the Penultimate Payment Certificate the Contractor shall pay the NN Sub-Contractor its Penultimate Payment being the sum due in respect of its Final Statement. If this differs from the sum claimed in the NN Sub-Contractor's Final Statement, the Contractor shall notify the NN Sub-Contractor of the differences and of the reasons for them.

(2)   At the time of the Penultimate Payment, if there are deductions which the Contractor intends to make from monies due to the NN Sub-Contractor [as provided for in clause 11(b) above] the Contractor shall give to the NN Sub-Contractor written notification of all such deductions not already notified in accordance with clause 11(b) above. Any such notification shall be given a reasonable time before the penultimate payment to the NN Sub-Contractor is due to be made.

(3)   In the event that, at the time of the Penultimate Payment, the total sum due from the NN Sub-Contractor to the Contractor (arising under sub-clauses 11(b)(1) and (2) hereof) exceeds the total of the sums due to the NN Sub-Contractor, there shall be a debt (for the difference) due from the NN Sub-Contractor to the Contractor. The NN Sub-Contractor shall pay such a debt within 7 working days of either the date when payment would otherwise have been due to the NN Sub-Contractor or of the notification by the Contractor of the debt, whichever is the later.

NOTE

The Employer's Representative is required by the Main Contract, to issue the Penultimate Payment Certificate within five months of the date of Substantial Completion of the Works. Within 20 working days of the issue by the Employer's Representative of the Penultimate Payment Certificate the Contractor shall pay the NN Sub-Contractor it's Penultimate Payment.

11(j)   Final Payment

The Employer's Representative is required, by the Main Contract, to issue the Defects Certificate within 20 working days of the end of the Defects Period (which may have been extended in accordance with clause 8.6 ("Defects Period") of the Main Contract). The Employer's Representative is required, by the Main Contract, to issue the final payment certificate within three months of the issue of the Defects Certificate. Within 20 working days of the issue by the Employer's Representative of the final payment certificate the Contractor shall pay the NN Sub-Contractor its final payment which shall be the sum due under this Sub-Contract and will include the final payment of retention (if not previously paid), any amount due for additional works instructed after Substantial Completion, any amounts which were withheld from the Penultimate Payment and are now due and deduction of any sums due from the NN Sub-Contractor to the Contractor. The Contractor shall provide the NN Sub-Contractor with a statement with the final payment showing how the final payment sum has been computed.

11(k) Taxes and Interest

The provisions in relation to Interest, Valued Added Tax and Withholding Tax in clauses 11.6 ("Time for Payment and Interest"), 11.7 ("Value Added Tax") and 11.8 ("Withholding Tax") of the Main Contract shall apply mutatis mutandis to the Sub-Contract. In so far however as an entitlement to interest arises in relation to payments certified under the Main Contract, the NN Sub-Contractor will only be entitled to a fair and reasonable proportion of such interest, if any, as is recovered by the Contractor.

11(l) Monies held in trust

The sums paid by the Employer to the Contractor in accordance with the provisions of the Main Contract insofar as they are payable to the NN Sub-Contractor under this Sub-Contract are held in trust by the Contractor for the NN Sub-Contractor.

12. TERMINATION

12(a) Termination on NN Sub-Contractor Default

The Contractor may, without limiting any other rights or remedies, terminate the Sub-Contract if any of the following occurs:-

(i) the NN Sub-Contractor in breach of contract fails to comply with its obligations under the Sub-Contract and, if the failure can be cured, the NN Sub-Contractor has failed to cure it within 10 days of being requested to do so by the Contractor;

(ii) the NN Sub-Contractor abandons or suspends the execution of the Sub-Contract Works;

(iii) the NN Sub-Contractor fails to proceed regularly and diligently with the execution of the Sub-Contract Works;

(iv) the NN Sub-Contractor fails to provide or maintain the required insurances or performance bond;

(v) the NN Sub-Contractor or NN Sub-Contractor's Personnel has or displays a level of incompetence such that the warranty given by the Contractor in clause 2.5 ("Safety, Health and Welfare at Work Act 2005 and Safety, Health and Welfare at Work (Construction) Regulations 2006") of the Main Contract is rendered untrue or the NN Sub-Contractor's conduct is or has been such as to render the Contractor's warranty under clause 2.6 ("Ethics in Public Office") of the Main Contract untrue;

(vi) the NN Sub-Contractor or NN Sub-Contractor's Personnel has committed or caused the Employer or the Contractor to commit a serious breach of Legal Requirements;

(vii) the NN Sub-Contractor or NN Sub-Contractor's Personnel have committed a breach of the Safety, Health and Welfare at Work Act 2005 or any regulations or code of practice made under it;

(viii) the NN Sub-Contractor or NN Sub-Contractor's Personnel has not complied with the requirements of clause 5(c) hereof either (a) within 10 days after notice from the Contractor requiring a failure to be put right or (b) persistently;

(ix) the NN Sub-Contractor has sub-contracted all or any part of the Sub-Contract Works without the consent in writing of the Contractor;

(x) if any of the insolvency events referred to in clause 12.1 ("Termination on Contractor Default") of the Main Contract occur in relation to the NN Sub-Contractor. In this case, the Contractor will have the same rights and entitlements *mutatis mutandis* in relation to the NN Sub-Contractor as the Employer has in relation to the Contractor under clauses 12.1.2 and 12.1.3 of the Main Contract.

NOTE

Grounds for termination by the Contractor are as follows:

1. The NN Sub-Contractor in breach of contract fails to comply with its obligations under the sub-contract;

2. The NN Sub-Contractor abandons or suspends the execution of the Works;

3. The NN Sub-Contractor fails to proceed regularly and diligently with the Works;

4. The NN Sub-Contractor fails to provide or maintain the required insurances or performance bond;

5. Any of the NN Sub-Contractor's warranties given by the NN Sub-Contractor in clause 2.5 ("Safety, Health and Welfare at Work Act 2005 and Safety, Health and Welfare at

Work (Construction) Regulations 2006") or sub-clause 2.6 (Ethics in Public office) of the Main Contract are untrue;

6. Committed or caused the Employer or the Contractor to commit a serious breach of Legal Requirements;

7. Committed a breach of the Safety, Health and Welfare at Work Act 2005 or any regulations or code of practice made under it;

8. The NN Sub-Contractor has not complied with the requirements of clause 5(c);

9. The NN Sub-Contractor has sub-contracted all or any part of the Sub-Contract Works without the consent in writing of the Contractor;

10. Insolvency.

12(b) Consequences of Termination for NN Sub-Contractor Default

If the NN Sub-Contractor's obligation to complete the Sub-Contract Works is terminated under clause 12(a) hereof, the provisions of clause 12.2 ("Consequences of Default Termination") of the Main Contract will apply, *mutatis mutandis*, as between the Contractor and the NN Sub-Contractor as if all references to the Contractor therein were to the NN Sub-Contractor and all references to the Employer, or the Employer's Representative were to the Contractor. For the avoidance of doubt it is confirmed that references to Contractor's Things, Contractor's Documents, Works Items and Works shall be read as referring to NN Sub-Contractor's Things, NN Sub-Contractor's Documents, Sub-Contract Works Items and Sub-Contract Works respectively and that like terms applicable to the Main Contract will be changed, where the context admits or requires, to meet the purpose and intent of this Sub-Contract.

NOTE

The consequences of termination for NN Sub-Contractor default are:

1. The NN Sub-Contractor leaves the site in an orderly manner;

2. Payment of any monies due to the NN Sub-Contractor are postponed and the Contractor shall not be required to make any further payment to the NN Sub-Contractor except as provided in this clause;

3. The Contractor as soon as practicable make an assessment of the amount due to the NN Sub-Contractor in respect of works completed in accordance with the contract and unpaid. This is the *termination value*;

4. The NN Sub-Contractor cannot remove any work items or things from the site unless instructed to do so by the Contractor;

5. The Contractor may engage other Sub-Contractors, use any work items and NN Sub-Contractor's things on the site and do any thing necessary for the completion of the works;

6. If instructed by the Contractor, the NN Sub-Contractor shall assign to the Contractor, without further payment, the benefit of any sub-contract, contract for supply, or other contract in relation to the performance of the works;

7. The Contractor may pay to any Sub-Contractor or supplier to the NN Sub-Contractor any amount due to it that the Contractor certifies as included in any previous interim payment. The NN Sub-Contractor shall re-pay to the Contractor such an amount on request;

8. The NN Sub-Contractor provides to the Contractor all Work Requirements and NN Sub-Contractor's documents.

9. When the works have been completed and the termination amount has been assessed, the Contractor shall certify the *termination amount* setting out:

    i.   The Contractor's additional cost of completing the works compared with the cost that would have been incurred if the works had been completed by the NN Sub-Contractor;

    ii. Loss and damage incurred by the Contractor as a result of the termination and its cause;

    iii. Amounts due to the Contractor by the NN Sub-Contractor.

If the *termination amount* is less than the *termination value* the NN Sub-Contractor shall raise an invoice for the difference and the Contractor shall pay that amount within 15 days of receipt of the invoice. If the *termination amount* is more than the *termination value* the NN Sub-Contractor shall pay to the Contractor the difference within 10 working days of receiving the Contractor's demand for payment.

12(c) Termination of the Contractor's Employment under clause 12.1 ("Termination on Contractor Default") of the Main Contract

(1) If the Contractor's employment is terminated by the Employer under clause 12.1 ("Termination on Contractor Default") of the Main Contract, this Sub-Contract will automatically terminate.

(2) If the validity of such termination is not disputed by the Contractor under the disputes resolution provisions of the Main Contract, or if it is disputed but the right of termination is upheld by a binding decision of a conciliator or arbitrator or court, the Contractor will indemnify the NN Sub-Contractor in relation to all loss and damage incurred by it by reason of the termination.

(3) If the validity of the termination is successfully disputed by the Contractor with the effect that the Employer is held by a binding decision of a conciliator, arbitrator or court not to have been entitled to terminate, the Contractor shall take whatever steps are reasonable to recover any losses sustained by the NN Sub-Contractor on foot of the termination and will pay to the NN Sub-Contractor the proportion of any sum recovered from the Employer in relation to the termination as is referable to the NN Sub-Contractor's losses or, in the event of a settlement or outcome to the dispute does not clearly define the sum payable in relation to the NN Sub-Contractor's losses, such proportion of the sum recovered by the Contractor as is just and reasonable in all the circumstances. In assessing what is just and reasonable, regard will be had to any reduction in the amount which might have been otherwise recoverable by the Contractor against the Employer as a result of clause 12.9 ("Reference to Conciliation") of the Main Contract. The Contractor shall provide such information as is reasonably required by the NN Sub-Contractor to demonstrate the Contractor's compliance with this clause.

12(d) Termination by the NN Sub-Contractor

The NN Sub-Contractor shall be entitled to terminate the NN Sub-Contractor's obligation to complete the Sub-Contract Works by notice to the Contractor in writing if any of the following occur:-

(i)   the NN Sub-Contractor has suspended the execution of the Sub-Contract Works for 15 working days in accordance with clause 11(d) hereof and the Contractor has still not paid.

(ii) work has been suspended by direction of the Employer's Representative under sub-clause 9.2 ("Suspension") of the Main Contract and a right to terminate has arisen in favour of the Contractor under that sub-clause

(iii) the execution of the Sub-Contract Works or a substantial part of the Sub-Contract Works has been suspended for a period of at least three months as a consequence of loss or damage that is at the Employer's risk under clause 3.1 ("Employer's Risks of Loss and Damage to the Works") of the Main Contract

(iv) an event or circumstances outside the control of the parties makes it physically impossible or contrary to Law for the NN Sub-Contractor to fulfil its obligations under the Sub-Contract for a period of at least six months.

(v) If the Contractor becomes insolvent as defined in clause 12.1.1 (11) of the Main Contract and the Employer has not terminated the Main Contract under clause 12.1 ("Termination on Contractor Default") thereof.

NOTE

The NN Sub-Contractor may terminate by notice to the Contractor if:

The NN Sub-Contractor has suspended the Sub-Contract Works for 15 working days in accordance with clause 11(d) and the Contractor has still not paid.

Work has been suspended by direction of the Employer's Representative under sub-clause 9.2 ("Suspension") of the Main Contract and a right to terminate has arisen in favour of the Contractor under that sub-clause.

Work or a substantial part of it has been suspended for a period of at least three months as a consequence of loss or damage that is at the Employer's risk under clause 3.1 ("Employer's Risks of Loss and Damage to the Works") of the Main Contract

An event outside the control of the parties makes it physically impossible or contrary to Law for the NN Sub-Contractor to fulfil its obligations for a period of at least six months.

If the Contractor becomes insolvent.

12(e) Consequences of Termination by NN Sub-Contractor or at Employer's Election

(1) If the Employer terminates the Main Contract under clause 12.5 ("Termination at Employer's Election") of the Main Contract that termination will automatically terminate the employment of the NN Sub-Contractor. In that event, or in the event of the NN Sub-Contractor terminating the Sub-Contract under clause 12(d)(i), (ii), (iii) or (iv) hereof, the following shall apply:-

(i) The NN Sub-Contractor shall leave the site in an orderly manner and remove any NN Sub-Contractor's Things

(ii) The NN Sub-Contractor shall give the Contractor all Works Requirements and all NN Sub-Contractor's Documents

(iii) The NN Sub-Contractor shall as soon as practicable provide to the Contractor a statement of the total of the following (the **termination sum**):-

- the unpaid value of the Sub-Contract Works completed to the date of termination and valued in accordance with clause 11(a) hereof

- the NN Sub-Contractor's reasonable costs of removal from the Site as a consequence of the termination

- all other amounts due to the NN Sub-Contractor under the Sub-Contract (but not damages)

The Contractor will take all reasonable measures to recover for the NN Sub-Contractor from the Employer payment in respect of the Sub-Contract Works and shall pay to the NN Sub-Contractor a fair and reasonable proportion of any sum recovered by the Contractor from the Employer in relation to the termination. If the termination sum indicates that money is due by the NN Sub-Contractor to the Contractor, the same will be paid forthwith by the NN Sub-Contractor to the Contractor. The Contractor shall provide such information as is reasonably required by the NN Sub-Contractor to demonstrate the Contractor's compliance with this sub-clause.

(2) Termination by the NN Sub-Contractor under clause 12(d)(i) or (v) constitutes a termination by reason of the Contractor's default or breach of contract and the NN Sub-Contractor will be entitled to be compensated in accordance with 10(c)(1) hereof.

> **NOTE**
>
> The following shall apply:
>
> The NN Sub-Contractor shall leave the site in an orderly manner and remove any NN Sub-Contractor's Things;
>
> The NN Sub-Contractor shall give the Contractor all Works Requirements and all NN Sub-Contractor's Documents.
>
> The NN Sub-Contractor shall as soon as practicable provide to the Contractor a statement of the total of the following (the termination sum):
>
> • the unpaid value of the Sub-Contract Works completed to the date of termination;
>
> • the NN Sub-Contractor's reasonable costs of removal from the site as a consequence of the termination;
>
> • all other amounts due to the NN Sub-Contractor under the Sub-Contract (but not damages).
>
> The Contractor will take all reasonable measures to recover for the NN Sub-Contractor from the Employer payment in respect of the Sub-Contract Works and shall pay to the NN Sub-Contractor a fair and reasonable proportion of any sum recovered by the Contractor from the Employer in relation to the termination.
>
> Termination by the NN Sub-Contractor under clause 12(d)(i) or (v) constitutes a termination by reason of the Contractor's default or breach of contract and the NN Sub-Contractor will be entitled to be compensated in accordance with 10(c)(1).

12(f)   Survival

Termination of the NN Sub-Contractor's obligation to complete the Sub-Contract Works shall not affect the NN Sub-Contractor's obligations under the Sub-Contract, (other than the obligation to complete the Sub-Contract Works, after termination) and in particular the obligations of the Contractor which survive the termination of the Main Contract under clause 12.7 ("Survival") thereof shall continue to apply to the NN Sub-Contractor, in so far as they relate to the Sub-Contract, after termination.

13. DISPUTES

13(a) Notice to Refer

(1) If a dispute arises between the parties in connection with or arising out of the Sub-Contract, either party may, by notice to the other, refer the dispute for arbitration by serving on the other a Notice to Refer. The Notice to Refer shall state the issues in dispute. The service of the Notice to Refer will be deemed to be the commencement of arbitration proceedings.

(2) If the Notice to Refer is served by the NN Sub-Contractor, and the Contractor is of the view that the issues in dispute relate in whole or in part to a dispute between the Contractor and the Employer, provided the Contractor so indicates by notice to the NN Sub-Contractor in writing within 21 days of service of the Notice to Refer, the dispute, as between the Contractor and the NN Sub-Contractor in respect of those issues will be dealt with under sub-clause 13(c) hereof.

> **NOTE**
>
> If a dispute arises between the parties in connection with or arising out of the Sub-Contract, either party may, by notice to the other, refer the dispute for arbitration by serving on the other a Notice to Refer. The Notice to Refer shall state the issues in dispute. The service of the Notice to Refer will be deemed to be the commencement of arbitration proceedings.

13(b) Conciliation

(1) Except to the extent that the disputes which are the subject matter of the Notice to Refer have been the subject of notice served by the Contractor under the preceding sub-clause 13(a)(2) hereof, no step will be taken in the arbitration after the Notice to Refer has been served until the disputes have first been referred to conciliation. Either party may activate the conciliation process by seeking the appointment of a conciliator at any time after the expiry of 21 days from service of the Notice to Refer. During that period of 21 days either party may give notice to the other of further disputes and, if such notice is given, those further disputes will be deemed to be included in the reference to arbitration.

(2) If the parties are unable to agree a conciliator, a conciliator will be appointed by the President for the time being of the Construction Industry Federation. If there is a fee for making the appointment, the parties shall share it equally. Once a Conciliator has been appointed to a dispute between the parties, unless the parties agree otherwise, the same Conciliator shall deal with all other disputes between the parties, provided he/she is agreeable to do so.

(3) The provisions of sub-clauses 13.1.3 to 13.1.12 of clause 13.1 ("Conciliation"), of the Main Contract shall apply to the conciliation between the Contractor and NN Sub-Contractor (changing the word Employer to Contractor, the word Contractor to NN Sub-Contractor and the word Contract to Sub-Contract) with the exception of the final sentence of clause 13.1.9 (referral to arbitration following notice of dissatisfaction) and the second sentence of clause 13.1.10 (referral to arbitration of failure by one party to comply with a Conciliator's recommendation in respect of which neither party gave notice of dissatisfaction). Also, sub-clause 13.1.11 of the Main Contract will only apply if either or both of the parties has given notice of dissatisfaction.

(4) If notice of dissatisfaction has been given as provided for in clause 13.1.9 (of the Main Contract), either party may proceed to have the issues the subject matter of the Notice to Refer resolved through arbitration.

(5) If a party fails to comply with a conciliator's recommendation which is binding, the other party may take such court proceedings as are appropriate to force compliance with the conciliator's recommendation without availing further of the conciliation or arbitration process.

NOTE

Any dispute can be referred to conciliation during the course of the contract. If the dispute is not resolved within 42 days after the appointment of the conciliator, the conciliator shall make his recommendation. The parties have 45 days to accept the recommendation. If the recommendation is rejected by either party the matter can be referred to arbitration.

If the recommendation stated that a sum of money should be paid by one party to the other then that shall be binding in the interim. The receiving party will have to provide a bond for the amount it receives.

Any dispute referred to conciliation shall be finally settled by arbitration subject to the arbitration rules stated in the works requirements.

There is no reference to appointing bodies.

13(c)   Joint Disputes

Any disputes the subject matter of the Contractor's notice under sub-clause 13(a)(2), hereof will be dealt with jointly with the dispute under the Main Contract on the following basis:-

(i)   the Contractor shall pursue the issue or issues in dispute under the Main Contract diligently

(ii)   The NN Sub-Contractor shall furnish the Contractor with all necessary information and documents in its possession in a timely manner and shall participate in and provide all necessary assistance for the preparation of submissions and pleadings and will indemnify the Contractor in respect of any loss or expense incurred as a result of the NN Sub-Contractor's failure to do so

(iii) the Contractor shall consult with the NN Sub-Contractor in regard to all pleadings and procedural matters in pursuing the dispute

(iv)   the Contractor shall ensure that the views of the NN Sub-Contractor in relation to the disputes, in so far as they relate to the Sub-Contract, are transmitted to any conciliator or arbitrator appointed in relation to the dispute and will, as far as practicable, safeguard the interests of the NN Sub-Contractor

(v)   the NN Sub-Contractor shall indemnify the Contractor in relation to any costs incurred in any such conciliation or arbitration to the extent that this is fair and reasonable having regard to the respective financial interests of the parties in relation to the issues in dispute and all other relevant circumstances. The NN Sub-Contractor will make such payments on account as the conciliation or arbitration proceeds as are reasonably sought by the Contractor

(vi)   the Contractor and the NN Sub-Contractor will be bound by the outcome of any such binding conciliation or arbitration between the Employer and Contractor in so far as it relates to disputes connected with the Sub-Contract

NOTE

If the Notice to Refer is served by the NN Sub-Contractor, and the Contractor is of the view that the issues in dispute relate in whole or in part to a dispute between the Contractor and the Employer, provided the Contractor so indicates by notice to the NN Sub-Contractor in writing within 21 days of service of the Notice to Refer, the dispute, as between the Contractor and the NN Sub-Contractor in respect of those issues will be dealt with under sub-clause 13(c).

13(d)   Arbitration

(1)   Except in the case of a dispute to which sub-clause 13(c) hereof applies, the parties shall jointly appoint the arbitrator and, if the parties are unable to agree an arbitrator to be appointed under this clause, the arbitrator will be appointed by the President for the time being of the

Construction Industry Federation. The appointment of a conciliator or arbitrator when Clause 13(c) applies will be made in accordance with the Main Contract.

(2) Any arbitration [other than under clause 13(c) hereof] between the Contractor and the NN Sub-Contractor will be governed by the Arbitration Procedure 2000 published by Engineers Ireland and will be subject to the Arbitration Acts 1954–1998.

NOTE

In the absence of agreement by the parties, appointments of arbitrators will be made by the President for the time being of the Construction Industry Federation. The appointment of conciliators and arbitrators for disputes under sub-clause 13(c) shall be made in accordance with the Main Contract.

Arbitrations (other than under clause 13(c)) shall be governed by the Arbitration Procedure 2000 published by Engineers Ireland.

APPENDIX

PART 1
to be completed by Employer before tenders are invited

A MAIN CONTRACT

The Main Contract Conditions are ....
....
....
Agreement Recitals Item A

> **NOTE**
>
> This sets out what the conditions of the **Main Contract** are.

B SUB-CONTRACT DOCUMENTS

Additional Documents relating to the Sub-Contract Works
Article 5 of Agreement
<u>NOTE:</u> *If there are any Novated Design Documents which pertain to the Sub-Contract Works, they should be listed here.*

1. ....
2. ....
3. ....
4. ....
5. ....

> **NOTE**
>
> Any additional documents relating to the sub-contract works are listed here. Reference is made to Article 5 of the Agreement and states that any Novated Design Documents which pertain to the sub-contract works should be listed here.

C INSURANCES

Public Liability and Employer's Liability Insurance
Clauses 3 (d) (2) and 3 (d) (3)

Minimum indemnity limits for public liability and employers' liability insurance:

- public liability insurance: €............................. for any one event, but this limit may be on an annual aggregate basis for products liability, collapse, vibration, subsidence, removal and weakening of supports and sudden and accidental pollution. (If not stated, €6,500,000).

- Employer's liability insurance: €............................. for any one event. (If not stated, €13,000,000).

Maximum excess for Insurance:

- public liability: €... in respect of property damage only (If not stated, €10,000). There shall be no excess for death, injury or illness.

- employer's liability: no excess.

Permitted exclusions from the Insurances:

The NN Sub-Contractor's insurance policies may include only the exclusions permitted Under the Main Contract as detailed in the Schedule Part 1 D thereof.

Professional Indemnity Insurance
Clause 3 (e)

Professional indemnity insurance is/is not (*delete one*) required. (If neither deleted, professional indemnity insurance is not required). If required, the professional indemnity insurance is to be kept in place for .... years after Substantial Completion of the Works is certified by the Employer's Representative (If not stated, 6 years). If Professional Indemnity Insurance is required, the minimum indemnity limit for professional indemnity insurance shall be €........................ for each and every claim or series of claims arising from the same originating cause/annual aggregate limit (*delete one*). The maximum excess shall be €..................... (If none stated, €50,000).

> **NOTE**
>
> Details of the insurance requirements under the contract will be listed here, Public/Products Liability, Employer's Liability Insurance, Public Liability Insurance, Private/Commercial Motors, and other ancillary covers. Professional Indemnity may be required and is referred to under clause 3 (e) on page 11 of the conditions.
>
> Reference is made to permitted exclusion from insurances, and reference is made to the Schedule, Part 1 D of the Main Contract.

D   THE SITE
Clause 7 (c)

Method of Measurement:
The Method of Measurement defining the general attendances is
.... [8]
(if left blank, the Method of Measurement (if any) defined in the Schedule part 1 B of the Main Contract will apply or (if none so defined) the Method of Measurement most commonly used in Ireland for the type of work being constructed in this case.

Special Attendances to be provided by the Contractor:-

1.   ....
2.   ....
3.   ....
4.   ....
5.   ....

> **NOTE**
>
> The Method of Measurement is specified and the (NN) Sub-Contractor should list any special attendances to be provided by the main Contractor.

---

[8] This should be the same as the Method of Measurement (if any) specified in the Schedule Part 1 B of the Main Contract.

E TIME AND COMPLETION

Starting Date
Clause 9(a)

Period following receipt of a written instruction from the Contractor within which the Sub-Contractor must commence work on site .... working days (if left blank the period is 10 working days)

NOTE

This section provides the Starting Date in accordance with clause 9(a). The NN Sub-Contractor shall commence work within the specified period of receipt of a written instruction from the Contractor. If there is no time specified in the sub-contract then 10 working days applies.

VERY IMPORTANT NOTE

The Employer must also provide to tendering NN Sub-Contractors a copy of the completed Schedule Part 1 to the Main Contract.

NOTE

As the NN Sub-Contract document is a back to back document with the Main Contract, it is important that the relevant items on the Main Contract as contained in The Schedule Part 1 are provided to tendering NN Sub-Contractors.

PART 2
to be completed by NN Sub-Contractor and submitted with tender

ADJUSTMENTS TO THE NN SUB-CONTRACT SUM INCLUDING DELAY COSTS
Clause 10 (b) (5)

The NN Sub-Contractor's tendered hourly rates for labour and related costs [including PRSI, benefits, tool money, travelling time and country money]:

- Craftspersons   €.............. per hour
- General Operatives   €.............. per hour
- Apprentices   €.............. per hour

(If left blank, or stated as a negative value, read as zero)

The NN Sub-Contractor's tendered percentage addition for costs of materials..............%

The NN Sub-Contractor's tendered percentage addition/deduction for costs of plant................. %

All of the above shall include on-costs, overheads and profit, and exclude VAT. (If either of the above is left blank, read as zero.)

The NN Sub-Contractor's tendered rate of delay costs is €.............. excluding VAT per Site Working Day. (If left blank, or stated as a negative value, read as zero.)

If part 1K of the Schedule to the Main Contract states that separate rates are to be tendered for separate periods or parts of the Works, the NN Sub-Contractor's tendered rates are as follows:

<u>Period or part of the Works (part 1K of Main Contract)</u>   <u>Tendered Rate</u>

- ....   €.................. per site working day
- ....   €.................. per site working day
- ....   €.................. per site working day

NOTE

This will be completed by the (NN) Sub-Contractor and will be provided with the tender. This basically commits the NN Sub-Contractor to adjustments to the NN Sub-contract Sum including delay costs.

Clause 10 (b) (5) – Adjustments to the Contract Sum, requires the NN Sub-Contractor to complete this section. All in hourly rates for craft-persons, general operatives and apprentices will have to be completed. There are no differentiations in the categories of craft-persons or apprentices unless specifically requested.

Percentage additions to the cost of materials and plant will have to be quoted.

Sub-clause 10 (c) – Delay Cost, of the NN Sub-Contract requires the NN Sub-Contractor to state the amount per day he will be recompensed for delays. The figures will also be used by the Employer to establish the Most Economical Advantageous Tender. Therefore the opportunity of commercial gain is stymied by competition.

"Most Economical Advantageous Tender"

To establish the Most Economically Advantageous Tender, the Employer will add to the tendered sum the following figures that the NN Sub-Contractor has quoted for in his tender:

- A number of delay days multiplied by the tendered site daily delay cost;
- A number of hours for work persons multiplied by the tendered hourly rates;
- An amount for materials multiplied by the quoted percentage addition;
- An amount for plant multiplied by the quoted percentage addition;
- VAT.

PART 3

<u>PAYMENT GUARANTEE</u>

WHEREAS [   ] hereinafter called the "NN Sub-Contractor" has entered or will enter into a sub-contract with [   ] hereinafter called the Contractor for the completion of certain sub-contract works relating to [*Brief Description of Works*] **AND WHEREAS** it is a condition of the said sub-contract that the Contractor provides a guarantee to the value of 25% of the initial sub-contract sum.

At the request of the Contractor we, [   ] hereby guarantee to pay to the NN Sub-Contractor any sum due under the said sub-contract to the NN Sub-Contractor by the Contractor in the event of the Contractor failing to make payment thereof within a period of 30 working days after the issue by the Employer's Representative of a certificate under Clause 11.1.3 of the Main Contract or 50 working days after the due date for submission of the Contractor's Interim Statement under Clause 11.1.1 of the Main Contract (whichever is the sooner) and no claim shall be made under this guarantee until after fifteen have elapsed since the NN Sub-Contractor has served on the Contractor notice in writing of its intention to seek payment under this guarantee of the sum due. For the purpose of this Guarantee a sum will be deemed to be due if it is payable under the terms of the Sub-Contract over and above any valid deductions the Contractor is entitled to make. If the allegedly due debt is disputed by the Contractor the issue must be resolved through the disputes resolution procedure under Clause 13 of the NN Sub-Contract before any payment will be made under this Guarantee.

The Guarantor agrees that no event or circumstance whatsoever, including, without limitation, any variation or alteration to the terms of the sub-contract or any allowance of time thereunder, or any waiver, forbearance or forgiveness by the NN Sub-Contractor of or in respect of a payment by the Contractor shall in any way release the Guarantor from or reduce or effect its liability hereunder.

This Guarantee is a continuing security and shall secure the ultimate balance from time to time owing to the NN Sub-Contractor by the Contractor notwithstanding the bankruptcy, liquidation, amalgamation, reconstruction or other incapacity or any change in the Constitution or name of the Contractor **PROVIDED HOWEVER** this Guarantee will terminate three calendar months after the Final Payment Certificate has been issued by the Employer's Representative under the Main Contract except in relation to claims made prior to that date.

The construction, validity and performance of this Guarantee shall be governed in all respects by Irish Law and the Irish Courts shall have exclusive jurisdiction to settle any dispute which may arise hereunder.

PROVIDED HOWEVER the total sum payable under this Guarantee shall not exceed €
[euro].

Dated this   day of   2008

NOTE

This is the Payment Guarantee to be signed by the NN Sub-Contractor and the Main Contractor.

The Contractor undertakes to provide a guarantee to the value of 25 percent of the initial sub-contract sum. This will guarantee payment to the NN Sub-Contractor any sum due under the sub-contract:

- In the event of the Contractor failing to make payment within a period of 30 working days after the Employer's representative issues a certificate of payment under the main Contract;

- Or 50 working days after the due date for submission of the Contractor's Interim Statement under clause 11.1.1 – Interim Payment, of the Main Contract (whichever is the sooner);

- No claim shall be made under this guarantee until after 15 working days have elapsed since the NN Sub-Contractor has served on the Contractor notice in writing of its intention to seek payment under this guarantee of the sum due;

- A sum will be deemed to be due if it is payable under the terms of the Sub-contract over and above any valid deductions the Contractor is entitled to make. Any disputes must be resolved through the disputes resolution procedure under clause 13 before any payment will be made.

INDEX